A HERITAGE *of* flowers

A HERITAGE *of*
flowers

Old-fashioned flowers *for* modern gardens

Tovah Martin
with additional contributions from Gaia Books

PHOTOGRAPHS BY
David Cavagnaro

FOREWORD BY Barbara Segall

Gaia Books Ltd

The purple plumes of *Amaranthus caudatus*, love-lies bleeding, have been appreciated in gardens since the 17th century

A GAIA ORIGINAL

Books from Gaia celebrate the vision of Gaia, the self-sustaining living Earth, and seek to help readers live in greater personal and planetary harmony.

Editor	Charlie Ryrie
Design	Kitty Crossley
Production	Lyn Kirby
Managing Editor	Pip Morgan
Direction	Joss Pearson, Patrick Nugent

Directory compiled by Charlie Ryrie
with additional research by Tovah Martin

All photographs by David Cavagnaro

Copyright © 1999 Gaia Books Limited, London
Text copyright © 1999 Tovah Martin
Drirectory text copyright © Gaia Books Limited

Published in the United Kingdom by
Gaia Books Ltd, 66 Charlotte Street, London W1P 1LR
and 20 High Street, Stroud, Glos GL5 1AZ
Internet: www.Gaiabooks.co.uk

ISBN 1 85675 093 0
A catalogue record for this book is available in
The British Library

Printed & bound in Singapore by Imago

10 9 8 7 6 5 4 3 2 1

THE AUTHOR
Tovah Martin is known throughout North America as a lecturer, writer, columnist and TV gardener. She is the author of several gardening books, including Tasha Tudor's Garden, for which she received the Garden Writer's Association of America's award for Best Book of the Year in 1995. She lives in Connecticut, in a historic home with a cottage garden filled with old-fashioned flowers.

THE PHOTOGRAPHER
David Cavagnaro is a naturalist, plantsman, writer and photographer whose words and pictures have appeared in books and magazines worldwide. His house in Iowa lies among acres of meadows which he has reclaimed from arable land to turn into a wildflower paradise, and his own large gardens are filled with heirloom flowers and vegetables.

THE CONSULTANT
Barbara Segall is a gardener and author of a number of acclaimed books on aspects of horticulture, consultant for many more, editor of the Herb Society magazine and chairman of the Garden Writers Guild.

CONTENTS

FOREWORD

If you look at a number of gardens on the same day you will probably see a range of similar plants, allowing for a variation due to individual preferences. You could say that our gardens, in effect, are snapshots of particular plants on particular days in time. Another time, another day, another garden owner and the picture might be different.

We each have our own favourite flowers, some of them remembered from a grandparent's or a parent's garden. Perhaps these plants are still popular and easy to find in garden centres, but if not, you may discover in your quest for the flowers of your particular and individual heritage, that they have disappeared from current garden commerce. This may be your first taste of what many discerning gardeners have experienced down the centuries: not only are plants in the wild endangered, but our garden plants too may be endangered species, varieties and cultivars.

John Parkinson, 17th century apothecary to James I and author of *Paradisi in Sole, Paradisus Terrestris*, was one such gardener who recorded the loss of flowers from remembered gardens of his youth. Once in popular currency, many of these flowers are swiftly lost once they go out of fashion. There may be several reasons for their decline. Perhaps they were difficult to propagate and multiply for commercial purposes – now with modern technology to hand that reason might not prevail. Perhaps they were victims of fashion and have fallen from favour, so nurserymen stop holding stocks of them and they disappear. Perhaps, more simply, pest and disease has reduced their numbers and they were considered difficult to keep going. In many cases plants have disappeared because the nursery that developed them declined and disappeared.

In any case, should we bother about them? After all, next year's flowers may be brighter, flower longer, have shorter stems, be more disease-resistant and perform well in our windy, wet summers! Of course we need to bother. Many gardeners may not be aware of the important role, beyond providing them with pleasure, that their gardens have. Our gardens hold plants descended from those that plant hunters and explorers endured all manner of danger to obtain. They hold plants that are the result of years of breeding and painstaking hybridisation. In essence our gardens are the repository of a rich and varied horticultural history and possibly, even today, hold some of horticulture's lost treasures.

How do garden plants acquire such high status? It doesn't matter how modern or up-to-the-minute our plants are, they have, at one time or another, in the distant or recent past, entered our gardens from the wild. Plant hunters, explorers, soldiers and botanists are among the people who have brought plants to and from various countries and ultimately into our gardens. Usually the first staging post on a plant's journey from one country to another was the Physic or Botanic Garden, where it was assessed for its economic, medicinal or culinary use. Those criteria have more recently been extended to include the plant's qualities as an ornamental garden plant.

Over the years these wild plants, whether native or exotic imports, have attracted the attentions of nurserymen and plant breeders, as well as amateur growers. Between them they have selected countless seedlings and plants, raised and developed hybrids and cultivars. In the beds and borders of gardens all over Britain many of their plant-descendants still still exist, staking their claim to a piece of garden history. Much accurate knowledge of plant history dates to the 1500s when many reliable herbals, catalogues and plant lists were circulated. Undoubtedly plant history existed before this but illustrations at this time became more accurate and less symbolic.

Old garden plants and historic gardens became serious subjects of study in the late nineteenth century. The cottage garden was perceived to be the repository of many so-called lost flowers. In fact, many of what we might now describe as old-fashioned, heritage plants survived, because they were what gardeners call 'good doers' and because they were the handed-down favourites of the ordinary, probably poorer, cottage gardener who didn't change his garden as often as the richer, more fashion-oriented upper class gardener might have done.

During the 1950s garden history and plant conservation began to interest a great many gardeners. Their concerns coincided with a much larger one: that for environmental loss of habitat and of the disappearance of many plants from their natural sites. In some cases species were surviving in gardens and not in the wild. Foremost in the field of this area of conservation or what it describes as the "hitherto untapped wealth of the vast genepool of plants cultivated in the British Isles" is the National Council for the Conservation of Plants & Gardens (NCCPG). Set up some 20 years ago, the NCCPG has, through its National Collections Scheme, the responsiblity for and care of some 600 collections of garden plants, involving 50,000 species and cultivars. Many of the Collections are duplicated, protecting the gene pool even further against the twin ravages of man and nature.

The NCCPG was born out of the 1972 United Nations Stockholm Conference on the Human Environment, and on its inception in 1978/79 identified in its Pink Sheet plants that were endangered. Through its Collection Holders and enthusiastic membership it has brought back into commerce many of the 'once-disappeared' plants.

Notwithstanding the NCCPG's short lifespan, there have been numerous success stories. Among them is the gaily striped red and white *Dahlia* 'Union Jack', first raised in Britain in 1911, lost and then discovered in 1996 in a Buckinghamshire garden. *Syringa* x *chinensis* 'Duplex', raised by the great French nurseryman Lemoine and thought to have been out of cultivation for at least a century, was reintroduced from the Ukraine via Denmark. The return to commerce of the evocatively fragranced, blowsy looking Malmaison Dianthus Collection, is yet another of the triumphs of NCCPG collection holders. Our gardens are the richer for their activity.

It is estimated that there are 404,694 hectares (nearly one million acres) of gardens in Britain, hundreds of thousands more across Europe. Each one of us then has a part to play in keeping old varieties and cultivars alive in our gardens, enriching our own enjoyment and increasing the biodiversity of the genepool of our plant heritage. All gardeners have an important role to fulfil in the conservation of this living germplasm, wherever they live and garden. Bear this in mind, particularly if you move to an old house with a mature garden. Wait a full year before you remove any of its plant contents. That way, as the seasons unfold you can discover what treasures it might hold.

Instead of seeking new plants from an already depleted natural environment, we should now encourage growers and nurserymen to offer us as wide a selection of plants as possible from the existing genepool of our gardens, and to seek out and re-discover those lost plants of previous generations. In *A Heritage of Flowers* Tovah Martin reveals the fascinating histories of many of our favourite heirloom flowers. Grow them and pass them along to the gardeners of the future.

Barbara Segall 1998

SPECIES, VARIETIES, CULTIVARS AND HYBRIDS

Flowers behave in certain ways depending on whether they are species, varieties, cultivars or hybrids.

SPECIES
Many important members of our floral heritage are species: the pure plants before birds, bees or humans start to meddle with them. Species occur naturally in the wild. Known or unbeknownst to man they existed long before people started to bring plants into gardens, predating the advent of botany.

When taxonomists started naming plants, they affixed Latinised binomials to species, such as Alchemilla mollis, Campanula glomerata, Dicentra spectabilis. *The seed of species will come true when planted.*

VARIETY
Some treasured old plants are varieties, that is, they occur in nature, and they're similar to a species but they have some defining trait differing from the species — perhaps white flowers such as the bleeding heart Dicentra spectabilis alba, *or naturally occurring double flowers such as* Campanula persicifolia flore pleno. *Although they are occasionally weaker than the species itself, they will come true from seed if segregated from other species and varieties.*

CULTIVAR
Here's where humans and other pollinators step in. A cultivar is a cross between two plants of the same species, either due to the actions of plant breeders, or sometimes due to the work of insects or the wind. They are named with the species followed by the specific name, such as Campanula glomerata *'Crown of Snow'.*

The seed of a cultivar will often appear to come true, especially if it is an old-fashioned cultivar that has been grown for many generations, but some seed is eventually likely to revert to the species type, so cultivars must ultimately be propagated vegetatively.

HYBRIDS
When plants from two different species or genera are crossed, a hybrid results. Seed from the resulting progeny will not produce plants with the same characteristics as their parents, and seed may not even be fertile.

SELECTIONS
Many old-fashioned flowers came to us through the selection process. An excellent example is the work that the Vicar of Shirley, Reverend W. Wilks, performed with poppies in the 1880s. One day, in a cornfield near his churchyard, he noticed a scarlet poppy Papaver rhoeas *with a white edge to its petals. He returned when seed was ripe, collected it and sowed it. He continued along the same vein for several seasons, removing any ordinary poppies that polluted his crop, and over a number of years he managed to stabilise a reliably white-edged strain of poppies, known as Shirley poppies. If you purchase a packet of Shirley poppies, those plants will have the same traits that the Reverend Wilks selected.*

Part One

Our floral heritage

1

What are "heritage" flowers?

People have always loved flowers. They have been universally appreciated, through every culture, in every age. There are no records of specific gardens before the second millennium BC but flowers were used as motif and ornament long before that, significant in religion and ritual, and decorating pottery, buildings and jewellery in East and West.

Some of the flowers we grow in our gardens have been grown for centuries, even millennia, others have been grown for decades, others are new - thousands of new cultivars are produced every year to tantalise gardeners. Some old flowers are not, and have never been, threatened, but others have been lost for ever or are in danger of extinction. This is particularly true of plant cultivars that had fleeting popularity at a certain point in history, superseded when new forms arrived on the market.

Flowers do not have to be ancient in order to be valuable, nor do they have to be original species. Some flowers that should be sought out and treasured were once natural quirks

ABOVE: Bedding violas were developed from pansies crossed with *V. cornuta* and *V. lutea* from Western and Central Europe

LEFT: The exuberant Oriental poppy came to North America from Armenia via France early in the 18th century

of nature; other beautiful but now endangered flowers were created by eager hybridisers in the 18th and 19th centuries, others are more recent. And it is at least as important to conserve wild flowers as cultivated varieties; some rather insignificant looking species may have qualities worth preserving for the future health of the plant and human kingdoms.

It is impossible to define exactly what constitutes a heritage flower, but once you begin to grow old-fashioned varieties in your garden certain traits will usually emerge. There are often differences in colours and forms as many old flowers exhibit simpler shapes and subtler shades, with less restrained habits. One often-noted difference is that early forms are often much more strongly scented than their recent counterparts – there is little comparison between modern long-stemmed carnations, for example, and the heavenly clove scent that floats off the petals of many early cultivars. Older varieties may also be hardier and tend to be less prone to infestation by pests.

Delicate flowers of gypsophila – baby's breath – contrast with the generous blossoms of this beautifully scented 'Seven Sisters' rambler rose

WHOSE HERITAGE?

Flowers have moved around the globe, slowly at first, but at increased speed from the 12th century, with new introductions dashing around the world from the 17th century on. Our flower heritage does not only encompass our native flowers, but also flowers that have been widely cultivated in our country.

Until late in the Middle Ages (500–1400) in Europe the majority of people were acquainted only with the wildflowers indigenous to their region. Cultivated flowers were largely the province of the privileged, grown and used by wealthy people. That was understandable because the average citizen had little time for cultivating flowers when every ounce of energy was spent in trying to survive.

Plants only began to move freely around the world after the development of trade routes, but they had travelled before that time, on winds and tides, deliberately with conquering armies, and randomly transported in horses' hooves and wagon wheels and suchlike. These random introductions didn't always take hold, and weren't necessarily embraced. Most of the early plants that were deliberately carried from one place to another were useful herbs, vegetables or crop plants. Apart from native flowers, some of the oldest plants in cultivation are herbs. However we know that the Romans also dispersed many flowers through Europe; roses were very important to Roman society and they introduced *R. gallica* and *R. alba* types to Northern Europe, as well as Madonna lilies (they used the bulbs for food and medicine), forms of cultivated violets and periwinkle.

Following the fall of the Roman Empire, there seems to have been little development in Western plants or gardens until the 9th century. Charlemagne's *Capitulare de Villi*, *c*.800, documented the plants that should be grown in town gardens throughout his empire. Although

Heritage flowers don't all have to come from ancient history. Every generation has the chance of a greater plant heritage than the one that preceded it, as every decade brings some new and worthy introductions. It would be a tragedy to lose our most historic plants but we must also keep an eye on our more recent past.

It was fashionable for Romans to bedeck their halls with garlands of roses, and strew benches, tables and beds with rose petals. Some of those very early Rosa gallica and Rosa alba forms are probably still in cultivation, because generations of gardeners have loved the flowers.

However, much of gardening history is about perceived taste and fashion. Victorian gardeners were crazy about coleus, they hybridised hundreds. But fashions changed and coleus became deeply unfashionable in Europe although they are once again popular in the United States, where the only named cultivar to survive from the 19th century into the 1990s is 'Pineapple Queen'. Perhaps the cast-offs didn't boast great sun tolerance, or were dowdy compared to the latest introductions, but they had their virtues.

the list favoured fruit trees and herbs, flowers are headed by the Roman favourites of lilies and roses; other floral herbs include clary sage, bearded iris, garden mallow, rosemary, rue, southernwood and tansy. Contemporary gardeners also grew sweet violets *Viola odorata* and hyssop, poppies and corncockles, monkshood and lemon balm, along with native cowslips and primroses.

The development and expansion of trade routes and the establishment of the great monastic foundations marked a major change in fortune for flowers. Within the relative calm of their walled gardens, herbs such as chamomile, sage, lemon balm, yarrow, winter savory and betony, brought from Southern Europe, arrived on British shores and became essentials. A plant's fate was only sealed favourably if it could be put to service. Only the wealthy had pleasure gardens, growing sweet-scented flowers and herbs around a grassy lawn.

With the Crusades, numerous plants such as coronilla and gladiolus from the Mediterranean, hollyhocks from Persia and lavender from Spain began filtering into British gardens. However, these introductions were not spread among the general populace for decades or centuries, at first they were kept primarily cloistered in monastery gardens, or in the grand gardens of a very few wealthy people.

By the 16th century, well recovered from the turmoil of the aftermath of the Black Death, the economic and housing situations had changed in Europe, allowing more people to embrace flowering plants even if they might not be absolutely crucial to their family's well-being. Many pretty little flowers such as pulmonarias (lungwort) and honesty *Lunaria,* as well as clove carnations *Dianthus,* came into popular cultivation, although people still most often justified their inclusion into the garden for culinary or medicinal purposes. Some, such as honeysuckle and roses brought in from the wild, may have been grown primarily for their scent to disguise the household odours, although roses have always been popular garden flowers.

The British were by no means the first enthusiastic gardeners – we know that garden design and flower development had been important for centuries in the Middle East and the Orient, However, introduction dates traditionally mark the year that a plant arrived in Britain. Not only did British gardeners and herbalists faithfully document new botanical immigrants, but they also proved conscientious hosts when botanical strangers arrived on their shores. And they kept the chain moving, sharing their finds with other kindred spirits. The British were great adopters, employers, chroniclers, stewards and disseminators of new arrivals.

Exuberant canna lilies were highly popular in Victorian gardens, grown as exotic focal points in elaborately designed borders

AMASSING OUR HERITAGE

Not long after Europeans arrived in North America, this New World was explored for horticultural treasures, among other things. Some of the earliest and most fruitful collecting expeditions were accomplished by the John Tradescants, a father (1570–1638) and son (1608–1662) team. The Elder became a shareholder in the Virginia Company, receiving plants through their efforts. His son travelled personally to collect in Virginia. They were responsible for the introduction of plants such as the coneflower *Rudbeckia laciniata*, the Jamestown lily *Zephyranthes atamasca*, goldenrod *Solidago canadensis*, spiderwort *Tradescantia virginiana*, Prince's feather *Amaranthus hypochondriacus*, American cowslip *Dodecatheon meadia*, milkweed *Asclepias syriaca*, foamflower *Tiarella cordifolia*, yellow passionflower *Passiflora lutea*, Virginia creeper *Parthenocissus quinquefolia* and turtle head *Chelone glabra* as well as many other North American plants including trees such as the tulip tree *Liriodendron tulipifera*.

ABOVE: Many American plants including common milkweed *Asclepias syriaca* arrived in England via John Tradescant the Elder

John Bartram (1699-1776) and his son William (1739-1823) were also important early plant collectors, sending finds to their English liaison, Peter Collinson, a fellow Quaker and an astute businessman. He in turn disseminated the newly supplied American novelties amongst eager gentlemen collectors in Britain, from where they passed into wide circulation.

The exchange went the other way as well. The first Pilgrims to arrive in North America arrived with seeds of plants that they deemed critical for their survival. The emphasis was on vegetables, of course, but non-native herbs and flowers also arrived early on North American shores. As the years progressed and communication improved, more and more plants arrived, a trend encouraged by prominent globe-trotting citizens such as Thomas Jefferson. Through correspondence abroad, they heard of rarities that were arriving in Europe regularly from further and further flung places and were eager to pay the price necessary to receive the objects of their desire.

As technology improved, and with the introduction of glasshouses during the 18th and 19th centuries, tender as well as hardy plants were taken from their homelands to distant lands where they survived to become integrated into the cultivated landscape. In the early 1800s steam travel allowed increased quantities of plants to return with explorers from the tropics. This collecting was initiated and funded by wealthy aristocrats and monarchs, who had plants brought home to be treasured in their own personal botanical gardens, but eventually the hardier of the new arrivals filtered into the public domain. The most exotic and tender tropicals remained the preserve of wealthy citizens who could afford their protection in glasshouses over the winter, and tropicals didn't filter down to the general populace until the late 19th century when glass became cheaper and more readily available.

In 1976, an ornate but overgrown and forgotten tombstone was discovered in the old graveyard of a derelict church in Lambeth, East London. The tomb contained the remains of two great 17th century plant hunters, John Tradescant (the elder) and his son John Tradescant (the younger).

The former church building now houses the Museum of Garden History and the old graveyard has been transformed into a reproduction 17th century knot garden, using material which would have been available to the Tradescants. Some of the plants are native, but a significant number were introduced to Britain by the Tradescants.

21

Moss phlox *Phlox subulata,* growing here with vivid green *Euphorbia*, were introduced to England from North America in 1745

ESTABLISHING NEW SPECIES

An imported plant introduction can only take root, thrive and persist from season to season if it can tolerate the conditions in its new environment. Not all the green immigrants brought back by explorers found their adoptive home hospitable. Some tropicals simply curled up their roots and perished in their first bitter winter. Even when plants were housed indoors many exotics proved difficult to accommodate; this was partly because of the unreliable fits and starts of stoves in primitive glasshouses, but probably more because the British gardeners didn't understand the needs of the foreigners.

The plants that we now consider as heritage flowers are survivors. Many species have developed highly defined physical characteristics to deal with the climate at hand, and adaptation has led to some astonishingly handsome traits. Some species are equipped with small, waxy leaves as protection from burning sun if necessary, or they brandish big furry foliage to stop excessive water loss and to capture maximum light. They develop root systems to soak up tiny droplets of moisture if that's all nature normally provides in their native habitat, or they sink a network of roots adapted to aquatic conditions if they normally grow beside bogs. Some of the most fascinating plants come from challenging habitats, and their adaptations to survive these situations are feats of engineering.

Hybridisers work with plants to lengthen their stems or render them dwarf, but few man-made alterations can equal the incredible solutions that plants devise unaided to survive in a stressful environment. Flowers use all sorts of ploys including fragrance, gaudily coloured petals, long-throated blooms, pollen streaks or throat blotches to attract their pollinators. Leaves are shaped in forms likely to facilitate existence in the wild. Seed casings are often aerodynamically designed to disperse just where germination is likely to be effective. Seeds might be contrived to crack only when seared by fire or when dashed against rocks. Diversity makes the botanical world go round.

Plants that are deprived of rain for several months of the year sometimes develop bulbous or tuberous roots to store moisture. Desert plants often have plump, succulent leaves and stems to hold water when little is provided. Alpine plants tend to hug the ground with creeping stems and tough, little leaves to protect them from brutally windy conditions at high altitudes and minimise the moisture they'll need when wedged between rock crevices.

Mediterranean and arid-land plants often have small, aromatic leaves rich in essential oils. Scented leaves baffle predators, and the oils that evaporate in the heat of the sun linger briefly after sunset to act as a blanket, protecting the plant from the sudden temperature drop.

Regionality is a wonderful thing. Your local weeds might seem rather provincial compared to exotics from afar, but take a second look. Upon closer inspection, all sorts of hidden secrets might be revealed. And remember that those plants have adapted to living happily in your region.

But gardeners have traditionally hungered after plants from other lands, and there's nothing wrong with inviting strangers to dwell on your turf. But before you transplant an heirloom or sow its seeds, study its native habitat. Fads and fashions come and go, but if you're trying to grow a tender plant in a northern frost pocket you are going to have a struggle unless you can alter the conditions accordingly. Protection will help but it may not be enough to ensure health and prosperity. In addition to learning about the history of a newly adopted plant, study its habitat. Find out its soil preferences and the hours of sunshine it enjoys in its native region, and experiment. It may not be one for you.

RIGHT: Common desert plants, numerous species of cacti exist, all excellently adapted to thrive in arid regions

FASHION AND PLANTS

Fashion is a great dictator. It decrees the current style of architecture, design and couture. It alters the etiquette of dinner party conversations and sways the syllabus of university courses. Fashion sets the trends, and the scene changes accordingly. Ten years from now, cars might be bigger or smaller, they might be electric, solar-powered or rendered altogether obsolete, but one thing is certain – they'll be different from the way they were last year. We tend to associate the term "fashion" with skirt lengths and tie widths, but its influence reaches far wider.

Along with everything else, flowers have changed considerably with time. The hybrid tea roses or bright bedding plants so popular in 20th century gardens would certainly have seemed curious to the Romans, just as the limited range of flowers and slightly subdued palette of a Tudor garden might seem rather dull to the modern eye. When gardening is popular, the landscape changes drastically from one decade to the next, altered by the whims of fashionable ideas and current designers. Gardening is as subject to fashion as any other pursuit.

Flower fashions themselves are volatile, and the fluctuations of clothing styles have also sometimes had a very direct influence on flowers – if lapel buttonholes, for example, disappear from men's jackets, then boutonnières rapidly slip out of vogue; this means that cornflowers are no longer hybridised in petal colours or with stem lengths appropriate for that purpose. Camellia corsages were once worn at the waist to accentuate a lady's hourglass figure, but when fashions changed the corsage was positioned more prominently on the shoulder and composed of eye-catching blossoms such as orchids. If the flowers that were grown for specific purposes disappear, especially if they happen to be hybrids, there's little chance that they'll ever surface again. The quirk of nature that produced many-petalled parma violets is unlikely to happen twice. As far as flowers are concerned, tides of fashion can be unrelenting.

Old-fashioned sweet peas are descended from *Lathyrus odoratus*, sent to Britain from Sicily in 1699 by Father Cupani, a Franciscan monk

But although fashions have sometimes harmed flower futures, they have also led to all sorts of innovations. Fashions have sent explorers wandering around the globe, collecting tropical plants and introducing them to the hothouses of Europe and North America. Trends in garden design have increased the legions of roses, geraniums, tulips, hemerocallis, pelargoniums and many many other flowers; they have transformed lupins, foxgloves and verbascum and made it possible for all of us to choose from wide arrays of different colours and sizes. Fashion means that certain flowers come to the forefront to enjoy a flurry of hybridisation – even if only for a few brief years – and increasing interest in gardening means that the quantities of plants in cultivation increase accordingly.

In 1975, the first edition of *The Plant Finder* was published, a volume listing cultivars available in the United Kingdom, with their sources. The first edition listed 22,000 plants; now there are more than three times that number. However, every edition also describes the loss of several thousand cultivars: to some extent it is inevitable that some will be lost in species which are very popular and highly hybridised, and where new cultivars are also introduced. Similarly, if you happen to look through horticultural classifieds with any regularity, or if you read letters to the editor in your favorite horticultural periodical, you're bound to come across quite a few botanical losts and founds placed by gardeners.

It's part of human nature to prefer something that seems slightly better than standard, to seek out new plants. Many newer arrivals seem more beautiful than the original species. But don't throw out the flowers from the past; they are part of our floral heritage and they may swing back into fashion at any time. A flower's numbers may increase according to the whims of fashion, but they can equally easily slip into oblivion.

ABOVE: Native to China, hollyhocks *Alcea rosea* have been popular ever since their introduction to Britain in the 16th century

FASHION IN THE GARDEN

For centuries most plant development depended on fate, chance introductions or serendipity. In fact, plant breeding didn't begin in earnest until the ramifications of Mendel's famous pea experiments (published in 1865) truly hit home. Before that time, plants were selected for chosen traits. For example, seed was saved of a poppy discovered with a white hem around its edge and all its ordinary neighbours were destroyed until a stable strain of Shirley poppies was established. If gardeners were striving towards a specific goal, the process took many growing seasons. You chose plants that naturally portrayed the qualities that you needed.

However, every decade or generation prefers a different style of garden design, and garden fashions drastically affect the repertoire of plants on everyone's wish lists. In the 19th century nurserymen began seriously to breed new races of particular plants, to the advantage of those who followed the latest trends, but much to the detriment of the original species that parented the hybrids. Columbines, astilbes, pelargoniums, lupins, verbenas and many other popular garden plants have developed very differently from the original species. Few modern gardeners give the species garden space. The hybrids display "superior" qualities and their parents disappear from cultivation. Who wants to host an inferior form? Unfortunately, this has meant that the parents of many common garden hybrids are no longer available.

As easier modes of travel were introduced and plants increased, garden fads were adopted and abandoned with ever-increasing rapidity. At one time or another, Britain fell head over heels for knot gardens of herbs shorn to look like a carpet, formal gardens loaded with blossoms, landscape parks with very few flowers, "natural" gardens with native plants incorporated, ribbon borders composed primarily of annuals and

FASHIONABLE FLORISTRY

There have been times when cut flower fashions have also influenced floral changes. Short-stemmed blooms could be threaded into a buttonhole or tucked into a hat while formal bouquets and flowers for deeper vases needed longer flower stems. All common cut flowers – dianthus, sweet peas, violets and roses – were eventually bred or selected for long stems.

Thanks to florists, sweet peas now have large fluttery petals due to a quirk of giganticism that was nurtured and harnessed. Sunflowers come in a broad spectrum of colours, roses have stronger stems capable of keeping heavy buds from nodding, double bouvardias are readily available as are double pelargoniums with flowers that don't drop their petals when you carry them across the street.

Sometimes fashions work against florists – marigolds became such popular bedding plants that they lost their original long-stemmed form much loved by florists; cosmos seem to be moving toward shorter stems to fulfil the desires of landscapers. The violets that were once bred on a massive scale purely to supply the New York City opera crowd with nosegays eventually fell victim to disease and vanished from the many glasshouses that mushroomed in nearby suburbs for their cultivation.

Sunflowers *Helianthus anuus* have always exhibited highly variable forms

What's in a name?

Native to the United States, the sweetly scented *Phlox paniculata* wasn't greatly revered in its home country, but it was an entirely different story when it was introduced to Europe in 1730. Here phlox were seen as rarities and treasures, and they have remained popular in North European

increasingly passionate about the species. Phlox are abundant in her region because they happily survive northern Vermont's prolonged and tempestuous winters.

But starting and organising a collection of plants poses many problems, even when there's plenty of available

seed so easily. You get something that looks interesting, but it could be a hybrid seedling rather than a named variety." And there is precious little reference material – few farmers kept accurate records of the varieties they planted, and probably knew few of them by specific names.

Naming is often a problem for collectors of old-fashioned plants – even when plants do come with a recognised name tag, you can't always be sure that the name has not been changed over the years, and even the most careful research sometimes fails convincingly to identify certain cultivars and varieties. Rachel Kane calls her favourite 'Old Cellar Hole', because it was found in the abandoned cellar hole of a ruined house. It might be an old named variety, but it might have been created out of a chance crossing.

Of course collectors need to spend time poring over old catalogues and reference books, but even the most precise descriptions can sometimes be open to question. For example, different people have different interpretations of what the colour "rose-pink" might be. In other cases plants that might appear to be otherwise identical to those described in early references may reach your shoulders when they are described as "excellent for the front of the border".

To make things even more complicated, the same phlox that display certain characteristics when grown in Britain, for example, may be slightly different when grown in north eastern America, affected by climatic factors. Guarding old-fashioned plants is not always an easy task.

ABOVE: Phlox paniculata *is native through much of North America, but first recorded in Europe in 1730*

gardens ever since. They are stalwarts of many herbaceous borders as they flower late, in July and August, when many of the more spectacular summer flowers are dying down after their earlier summer glory.

Phlox have always grown so widely in cooler parts of North America that their value was scarcely recognised until recently. But some specialist nurseries and collectors such as Rachel Kane of Perennial Pleasures in East Hardwick, Vermont, are becoming

material. Much of Rachel's collecting takes place in Britain, virtually the only place where she can be certain of finding specific named varieties. In the 1940s, when phlox was enjoying its heyday, there were 202 named varieties of *P. paniculata*. In Britain the National Collection holders now keep 86 cultivars, while Rachel's catalogue now lists about 25 after several years of collecting and research.

The main difficulty for North American collectors is not the lack of collecting material, but it's hard to identify the plants with any certainty. "One of the troubles is that they set herbaceous borders full of perennials. There have been shrubberies, nutteries, pinetums and other favourites, or mixtures of different styles worked in tandem. And as each fashion waxed and waned different plants came into play.

The United States saw the coming and going of many of the same fads – usually arriving several years after climaxing in Europe. It is only recently that North American gardens have given space to their native plants. Instead, American gardeners have tended to follow foreign trends, whether they were pioneers with a few favourite flowers from their homelands, or wealthy later compatriots who invested considerable time and money to make their grounds blossom. Over the past 200 years, wealthy American gardeners have favoured Japanese gardens, Italian gardens, Elizabethan knot gardens and Spanish gardens. Colour theme gardens have had enduring popularity at different times.

Fashions continue to change: herbaceous borders make way for naturalistic planting; fiery colours usurp pastel shades; bedding plants and perennial gardens fall in and out of favour, shrubberies are turned over to grasses, and every gardening fad has its attendant flowers. As different gardening styles are embraced, new plants are made available to be dropped just as rapidly with the next fashion. And plants from the past get forgotten.

Whatever kind of garden you choose to plant, don't be too quick to throw out the old cultivars. Quite apart from questions of garden trends, old-fashioned flowers can often be raised from seed while many of the latest cultivars with stunning colour combinations can only be propagated vegetatively. In time cultivars raised vegetatively can succumb to illnesses, and for plants to remain healthy long term they may need to be replenished with seed-raised stock from time to time. The best way to ensure a healthy garden future may be to keep an eye on the past.

WHICH FLOWERS TO TREASURE?

A flower that may be considered special in your community may be ignored by another. Some of our favourite old-fashioned flowers are endangered, some are widely grown. Many historic flowers are species, but not all. Some of the earliest introductions had been subject to selection for centuries in the Far and Middle East before the plants were carried on trade routes. The first chrysanthemum to arrive in Europe from China was already far removed from the simple daisy-like *Chrysanthemum indicum*, which had seen human intervention since the T'ang Dynasty (618-906). The first azalea to come from China in 1808 was the wild scarlet-flowered form, but white, oranges, purples and doubles followed rapidly. And although simplicity is often a trait of ancient heirlooms, not all double flowers are new introductions. Double-flowered and striped camellias could be seen by the earliest explorers in China.

Broad sweeping generalisations are impossible, but a few traits recur in "heritage" flowers that are worth guarding. Scent is one of these, as old-fashioned flowers are often more fragrant than their modern counterparts, although some people disagree and say that modern roses, for example, can smell just as sweet. People have very different senses of smell. Colours are also often more subdued in older flowers; certainly old roses tend to have a more subtle blush than some of the newer hybrids. Old-fashioned flowers tend to be more disease resistant (although some plants such as hollyhocks or phlox are very prone to mildew or rust).

Apart from traditional garden plants, some native flowers are extremely rare in the wild and may rely on gardeners to survive. These are our real historic heritage and we must make sure we do what we can to preserve them.

2

Wildflowers: our earliest heritage

Long before gardeners tidied plants into gardens, people were picking handfuls of daisies and presenting them to sweethearts. Wildflowers were the first flowers everyone knew, the repertoire of familiar faces varying drastically depending whether you happened to live by the seaside, inland, on a mountaintop or in a valley. Your own region was special, it boasted its own distinctive flora and its own floral heritage.

Every region of the globe that can support animal or human habitation can also support plants specially adapted to surviving the conditions at hand. Call many of them weeds if you will, but wildflowers are survivors, brilliantly equipped to endure the rigours of their native domain. Adaptations are ingenious; some wildflowers brandish spines or thorns to fend off predators where forage is sparse, others have succulent leaves to retain water where rainfall is scarce. Meadow blossoms are large and colourful, the better to be singled out by roving butterflies, while alpine flowers often have modest, ground-hugging blooms that give off strong scent to attract their pollinators. Prairie flowers tend to be long-stemmed and wind-pollinated to take advantage of the gusts that whip through their native wide open spaces. Butterfly-pollinated flowers are usually bright, while night-blooming moth-pollinated flowers are generally luminous white. The variations and ingenuity of nature are endless and fascinating. Although there are undoubtedly many insignificant wildflowers on the globe, many are very handsome once you take a moment to focus on their charms.

Even common dandelions are splendid and complex plants, if you forgive the fact that they tend to monopolise your lawn. They are opportunists, but in the greater scheme of things, dandelions help ensure that every field is not a monoculture of grasses. The beauty of wildflowers lies in their multiformity, and the way each flower's unique peculiarities happen entirely independent of man. Nature is infinitely creative.

ABOVE: The dainty trout lily *Erythronium dens-canis* has been recorded in European gardens since 1596

LEFT: Wild forms of the water iris *Iris sibirica* have been found in many areas of Northern Europe for 500 years

The Mayflower story

Growing up in New England, I remember trailing arbutus, creeping around an old cemetery overgrown with trees and visited once or twice a year by someone with a scythe. The cemetery wasn't the most exciting place on Earth from most vantage points, but I would wander up there in spring, clear fallen leaves from the patch, sit on a toppled tombstone and commune with the Mayflower, trailing arbutus, *Epigaea repens*. The wildflower was insignificant for much of the year; its thready stems and battered little leaves didn't really beckon during June or July. But in May, every pink-lipped flower of that ground-hugging creeper held a whole perfume bottle of fragrance in its petals. I would crawl on hands and knees, bury my nose in the blossoms and inhale a breathtaking scent that lingered in my memory all year.

Arbutus featured in Native American folklore and legends. According to their lore, every spring, Seegun (the summer spirit) came to claim the earth from Peboan (the spirit of winter). As Seegun thawed the forest, Peboan slowly withered away until all that remained were the furs that he wore. From those furs, arbutus leaves sprang and Seegun nestled them into the soil, her warm breath forced the plants to blossom. Although patches of snow were still scattered throughout the forest, arbutus was a symbol that Seegun possessed the earth.

Trailing arbutus was abundant when the Pilgrims came to North America, dubbing it 'the Mayflower' in honour of its month of bloom and also to commemorate the ship that brought them to the New World. For centuries the little flower was prolific throughout woods in southern New England, where many people celebrated the first sunny days of spring by trotting off to find a patch of trailing arbutus in the woods, returning home with a bouquet of its aromatic blossoms. But that's where the problems began. With the Industrial Revolution people moved cityward, but memories of rural roots or traditions encouraged citydwellers to send peddlars and florists out to the woods to pick trailing arbutus wholesale and bring the flowers to the city. By the end of the 19th century commercial collectors had grown so greedy that several states deemed it necessary to pass laws protecting the plant. However the laws – largely unenforceable – were allegedly based primarily on sentiment as the Mayflower was still common enough in 1918 to be declared by Massachussetts their state flower.

At the same time, and more seriously, forests were slipping away. The Mayflower likes shade overhead and an acid soil rich in forest litter underfoot, and it often grew in association with chestnut trees, which disappeared rapidly after chestnut blight began its rampage through North America in the early 1900s. Well-meaning efforts to transplant *Epigaea repens* generally failed because of an essential symbiotic fungus clinging around the roots. It is nearly impossible to dig trailing arbutus without damaging the root fungus, yet without it the plants will die, starving to death before the necessary balance can be restored.

People foresaw the demise of the Mayflower, and in March 1925 Massachusetts attempted to save its floral emblem by passing an emergency law levying a $50.00 fine on anyone found collecting blossoms and a $100.00 fine on anyone collecting for profit. Even so, it was astonishing how rapidly the Mayflower slipped away. The Plant Buyer's Index of 1927 listed 25,000 plants of *Epigaea repens* available wholesale. By 1931, there were none on the market. Although the plant still exists, few New Englanders today have ever seen or smelled the Mayflower.

I consider myself fortunate to have a memory of its fragrance buried in my youth. Once an integral element of local folk heritage and spring traditions, the Mayflower, like so many others in our rich heritage of wildflowers, has disappeared into obscurity.

WILDFLOWER ROOTS

There are more than 200,000 vascular plants on the globe, and each and every one was once (and still might be) a wildflower somewhere. Ancestors of the pelargoniums that are coddled on windowsills run rampant around the Cape of Good Hope in South Africa. The poinsettias proffered at festivities grow unbidden in Mexico. Certain wildflowers are indigenous to only a confined ecological niche, too specialised to adapt comfortably elsewhere; others have been introduced into cultivation and nurtured in gardens beyond their native region. But many quietly remain wild, growing only in the woods, pools or rock outcroppings where they are happy. The least adaptable wildflowers are most prone to extinction.

The wildflowers that cast seeds and roots merrily over the broadest ranges usually enjoy the greatest popularity. They are the plants that figured strongly in folklore and custom to become part of the universal network of wildflowers. When a wildflower was recognised and loved by significant masses of people, many uses, legends and names grew up around that plant. Some of those customs and associations travelled broadly, others remained unique to an area. Dandelions were called pishamoolags in Ireland, dumbledores in Labrador, pissabeds in Newfoundland, dashalogas in Rhode Island, doonhead clocks in North Carolina, swine-snouts and witch-gowans elsewhere. Other wildflowers were known by even more numerous, but equally inventive epithets. Foxglove, for example, has answered to hundreds of common names throughout its long career, first as a wildflower and later as a cottage garden plant. The quantity of common names amassed by a wildflower gives you some indication of how broadly that plant spread and how beloved it was by the people – often also indicating that it was useful in home pharmacy or kitchen.

FOXGLOVES

At different times, in different parts of Northern Europe, foxgloves have rejoiced in the following names, some of which are still common: Bee catchers, Beehives, Blobs, Bloody Bells, Bloody Fingers, Bunny Rabbit Mouths, Clothes Pegs, Cowflops, Deadmen's bellows, Deadmen's fingers, Dog's lugs, Dragon's Mouth, Fairy Cap, Fairy fingers, Fairy's petticoats, Finger cap, Finger boot, Flop a dock, Flop-poppy, Fox-and-leaves, Foxflops, Granny's fingers, Gooseflops, Gapmouth, Hill poppy, King's Elwand, Lady's fingers, Lion's mouth, Long purples, Mary's candle, Popbells, Popdock, Poppers, Rabbit's flower, Scabbit dock, Scotch mercury, Snapjack, Thimble flower, Throatwort, Tiger's mouth, Virgin's fingers, Witch's thimble.

The foxglove was a fairy plant or a goblin's plant in England, Wales and Ireland, a plant of magic, with supernatural powers. Fairies were supposed to have given the corollas of the flower to foxes who wore them as gloves so as to sneak in magic silence up to poultry or away from hunters. Among their many powers, foxgloves were once considered able to bring back children taken away by the fairies.

In many country areas in Northern Europe foxgloves were used for centuries as a purge against fevers, colds and other illnesses.

LEFT: Foxgloves *Digitalis purpurea* have long been used in medicine   RIGHT: Soapwort *Saponaria* is still used in washing fragile textiles

ABOVE: Bluebells *Hyacinthoides non scripta* are now endangered in the wild   BELOW: Violets are among the 400 species in the *Viola* family

FROM FIELD TO STORE

By whatever names they were known, wildflowers were once integral to daily life. Most people were intimately familiar with their regional flora and knew the identity, blooming times and particular uses of their botanical neighbours. Individuals, families and whole communities interacted with wildflowers on a regular basis. They were woven into the thread of daily life. Not only were wildflower petals plucked to discern whether he loved you, or loved you not, wild plants were involved in many of the regular tasks necessary to stay alive.

Wild food was once an important way of surviving the dearth between the time the last potato was put on the table in late winter and spring and summer harvests. When people were starving, nettles and plantain leaves seemed a delicacy. By necessity, the average man, woman and child could readily distinguish between the poisonous Bad Henry *Mercurialis annua* and the similar looking wild salad herb Good King Henry *Chenopodium bonus-henricus*. This latter plant, and its many near relatives, now feature in upmarket vegetable seed catalogues, along with dandelions. Nowadays you can walk into an urban foodstore or fashionable restaurant to find that such plants have become fashionable ingredients, with purchasers paying a high premium for eating pre-packed purslanes or corn salads, or the rather unlovely samphire – all humble wild plants. The salad herb rocket *Eruca sativa,* which has been picked from the wild and eaten for centuries in continental Europe, is now a popular salad leaf sold by some English supermarkets at an astonishingly high price.

Some old wildflowers have been lost to time, and most of their uses long forgotten. Other ancient wildflowers undoubtedly also hold secrets yet to be rediscovered and harnessed. In Elizabethan times, in England, the salt-tolerant samphire, *Salicornia maritima*, was used as a potherb – Shakespeare mentions 'the dreadful trade' of harvesting samphire from the cliffs of Dover. Samphire can still be found around estuaries in some limestone areas, and it is now being studied as a possible food crop in desert regions where only brackish water is available for irrigation. Only 10 per cent of the world's flora has been tested for possible medicinal value. Fewer have been explored as food crops.

Until relatively recent times, every wildflower was part of the scheme, valued for its unique qualities; those that weren't edible were put to a multitude of other uses. The delightfully pungent leaves of ambrosia, *Chenopodium botrys*, were tucked into the folds of laundry as a moth-repellant. Some plants were woven into cloth – stinging nettles can produce a fabric more durable than linen. Detergents were made from many others including soapwort *Saponaria officinalis*, which is still used today to clean textiles in museum collections. Even more crucially, wildflowers have always been harvested to furnish medicines – even conventional medicine includes some form of plant drug in many prescriptions, and herbal medicine has never died out but is regaining popularity. We now know that many wild plants contain antibacterial, antifungal and antibiotic properties; others have sedative or stimulant qualities; others heal pain or restore energy.

Although there was a time when folk medicines required liberal gathering of plants, it is only recently that wildflowers have become increasingly threatened by disappearance and the trade in those required for medicinal use of necessity increasingly regulated. Some of the uses of wildflowers are only just becoming known, others are becoming better understood, so we must take care of them.

Much folk medicine is based on sound principles. For example elecampane (Inula helenium) and yarrow have been used to heal wounds for thousands of years: we now know they contain antibacterial, antifungal and antibiotic properties. Borage was encouraged early on from the wild into gardens as a cure-all, particularly valued to bring courage and dispel melancholy; research shows that it stimulates specific functions that prime the body for action in times of stress or danger.

In 1785 an early physician was believed to be given foxglove as a remedy by a witch. He then researched its properties to find that it acted upon the heart and was a good diuretic, establishing its future importance as an instrument against heart disease.

Digoxin derived from digitalis now saves thousands of lives every year. The ubiquitous garlic is antibacterial, antiviral, antifungal and antiparasitic.

STORIES AND SEASONS

Folk history was once as important in Western life as it remains today in less developed cultures. Legends explained the turning of the seasons, the creation of life and the forces of good and evil to people who had no understanding whatsoever of science. Flowers were given different attributes in different cultures. During the Middle Ages, foxglove was thought in some parts of the world to deter witches, and superstitious Welsh housewives later used a black dye of the leaves to paint witch-proof black lines on the stone floors of their cottages. In other parts of Britain, picking foxglove was thought to offend the fairies, with dire consequences. Garlic was introduced into England in 1548 from the Mediterranean, where it was considered an aphrodisiac, while in the Orient, that pungent wildflower was held at arm's length and believed to possess magical qualities. Much later, German miners brought garlic cloves when descending into the mines to ward off underground evil spirits.

Wildflowers also mark the seasons. Rhythms and cycles were once counted by blossomings rather than calendar dates. Once British countryfolk even used to tell the time by the pale blue flowers of wild chicory which open at 7 o'clock and close at midday. Where a wildflower was prevalent and its blossoming was a much-anticipated moment, festivals and holidays sometimes accompanied its blooming. In Britain, June 23rd was traditionally St. John's Day when garlands of St. John's wort, *Hypericum perforatum*, were hung on doors and windows as a talisman against evil. Superstitions may no longer be celebrated so outwardly, but wildflowers are still fêted as star attractions during seasonal festivals. It wouldn't be May Day without apple blossoms accompanying the festivities, and daisies are a crucial fixture in the USA on July 4th.

BELOW: Purple coneflowers *Echinacea purpurea* above globe thistles *Echinops ritro* ABOVE: Monarch caterpillar on *Asclepias tuberosa*

A striking dark form of the traditional cornflower *Centaurea cyanus*

WHERE ARE THEY NOW?

People tend to rally around the beady-eyed, soft and furry issues of habitat loss. We may mourn when a familiar flower slips away, yet countless specialised meek and mild wildflowers that most people never even encountered are also slipping away. The extinction of one single species of plant can confer the same fate on tens, hundreds or even thousands of animals, birds and insects. Even insignificant looking wild plants could possess virtues as yet unexplored. When plants disappear, however small their contribution was to our lives, it is a matter for concern.

Although wildflowers have been harvested for culinary, medicinal and other uses throughout history, sometimes in considerable quantities, most were still plentiful 250 years ago. But when populations shifted cityward the new concrete, plant-bereft domain left people with memories but infrequent access to the native blossoms that figured so firmly in ritual and legend. So wildflowers were brought to them. Eager customers paid florists to go into the woods and meadows and pick favourite blossoms or deliver pots of traditional symbols of spring into the great metropolises. That's when wildflowers began noticeably faltering.

The problem continues. In Britain, the bluebell *Hyacinthoides non-scripta* is one of the national symbols of spring, where whole tracts of woodland used to be carpeted in blue. In 1998 a law was passed to protect the once ubiquitous woodland flower; one contributory factor to its demise was the fact that it had been dug so relentlessly from its native habitats.

In Northern Europe deer and rabbit populations are at an all time high, devouring numerous wild plants and blamed for some disappearances. But the greatest of all current threats to wildflowers is habitat loss. The destruction of habitats has wreaked incredible havoc with the world's delicate balance.

WHY HAVE THEY GONE?

As human populations grow, agricultural operations have expanded. Large-scale agricultural development presents a worse evil than merely altering the land that it steals for its immediate operations. It impacts on a much wider area. Extensive and intensive agriculture has taken over much of the developed world in the last 25 years, with disastrous consequences for our native habitats. Ever larger fields are created and meadows and pastures reseeded with monocultures. Ancient hedges are ripped out to allow larger and larger machines to work the increasingly large fields.

As the rural work force has been replaced with contracted out labour, new workers arrive who do not have the same sense of place and permanence; crop rotation and fallow and mixed farming have been replaced with machines, chemicals and excessive use of fertilisers. Also, land has been drained on a massive scale to allow more intensive agriculture and to make it suitable for building. So old water meadows and farm ponds have disappeared, along with their wildflowers.

To survive healthily and fruitfully, many wildflowers require the stretching swathes of land that existed before the Industrial Revolution. Others need the cover of varied trees but native woodlands and coppices have been extensively replaced with exotic conifers, mixed hedges uprooted, and heaths, moorland, forest land and bogland have all been overgrazed where once wildflowers flourished. Moreover more and more roads have been built throughout the countryside dissecting viable populations of plants and the animals and insects which depend on them and on which they depend.

Side effects of agricultural intensification include additional pollution, herbicide run-off and pesticide drift. The wildflowers that survive its immediate encroachment are visited by fewer pollinators and sickened by chemicals.

There are other ramifications to population increase. People put up shopping centres, car parks and airports where wildflowers once reigned supreme. They want roads, leisure facilities, fuel, shelter, tennis courts and lawn-carpeted gardens. As a result, mining operations increase, suburbs sprawl, the natural environment dwindles – wildflowers are squashed and squelched.

In the United States, the imperiled Midwestern prairies tell a particularly poignant story of vanishing lands. Swallowed by agriculture, they are virtually gone. Meanwhile, Europe has even less in the way of natural vegetation left, with destruction of habitats escalating out of control in the last 50 years – Britain alone has lost 98 per cent of its native flower meadows, 60 per cent of its heaths, half its marshes and half its virgin woodlands in the last 40 years.

The numbers are frightening. Ten per cent of the world's flora is tottering on the verge of endangerment. In other words, of the 250,000 chronicled species of plants dwelling on the globe, 25,000 are imperiled. Many of these disappearances are occurring in the species-rich, yet over-exploited rainforests of the world, but a horrific number of losses are happening every day right under our own noses. While people are becoming increasingly aware of the plight of some of our most beautiful wildflowers, such as orchids, and of the healing potential of others, many stand no chance of surviving for future generations. Of all the tens of thousands of plants reputed to live somewhere on the globe, only a tiny number of those wildflowers have stayed around for centuries. It's tragic to think that fewer will still be there for future generations.

When we lose wildflowers we not only lose important botanical treasures, we also allow our local identity and culture to be diminished.

The smallest nature reserve in Britain, Badgeworth Pool in Gloucestershire, is dedicated to the conservation of the adder's-tongue spearwort, Ranunculus ophioglossifolius. This small-flowered and mud-loving annual could once be found in marshy areas of the Channel Islands as well as several southern English counties, but is one of the many floral tragedies of development, and its plight has not been helped by its very specific habitat and climate requirements. It needs bare soil from August to October to germinate the seed; a mild autumn to keep the ground moist – if frosts come early all seedlings die; plenty of rain in winter to submerge the plants – but not too much or they drown, and lack of severe frost or plants freeze to death.

Badgeworth Pool has been a reserve since the 1930s, withstanding threats of development and change of agricultural practices, but in 1973 it really hit the headlines when threatened by pollution from a neighbouring business. A fierce local campaign made the tiny buttercup into a national figure, and the "Badgeworth Battle" was reported as far afield as Missouri, USA.

Saved by the campaign, the little flower became a local hero, with the crowning of a "Buttercup Queen" a central feature of the local village fête.

The adder's-tongue spearwort now rests comfortably once again out of the public eye. Its flirt with fame may have been brief, but the dedicated action of local guardians has ensured that it should have a long and healthy future.

The giant helleborine orchid *Epipactis gigantea*

The showy orchis *Orchis spectabilis*

PRESERVING WILDFLOWERS

There is no easy solution, but you can help. Consider allocating an area of your garden to growing wildflowers. By adopting wildflowers, planting them and nurturing them, you shelter them from their precarious existence in the wild. You can help keep wildflowers from slipping into extinction. Although wildflower gardening doesn't take the place of habitat preservation, it helps wildflowers survive. And it renders them intimate, strengthening their bond with future generations.

Planting wildflowers is no new fad. Wildflowers were encouraged along roadsides as early as 1285 when Britain's anti-bandit laws were passed, stipulating that there could be no highwayman-hiding trees, bushes or ditches within 200 feet of roads linking market towns. Before sugar was imported, honey plants were cultivated to quell the driving hunger for sweets that has run constant throughout history. And long before exotics came into cultivation, people were nurturing such wildflowers as betony, geum, bellis, ajuga, chamomile, primroses, horehound, mugwort, foxglove, St. John's wort, herb Robert, wood sorrel, wild celery, vervain and agrimony in their gardens according to Mayster Ion Gardener, author of *Feate of Gardening* written in 1440.

Not all of those wildflowers remained solid fixtures in the garden, but many – bred to bear bigger, better flower trusses – have become common garden plants. Primroses, foxgloves, geums, violets and the like are now classified firmly as garden fare. They are now part of our cultivated floral history rather than the heritage of the field.

There may be nothing new about planting wildflowers, but wildflower gardening has taken on a dire immediacy in recent years as plants left to their own devices slip away. As long as the wildflowers sold for garden use are nursery propagated rather than dug from the wild, the trend has the firm support of wildflower organisations.

However, it isn't quite as easy as it sounds. Don't expect wildflowers to fend for themselves. Prepare the site, amend the soil and defend the site from encroachment of more aggressive weeds, just as you would maintain any planting. Although it sounds like a contradiction in terms, you can't just plunk wildflowers in the wild and expect them to survive. You've got to give them a fighting chance. The truth is that wildflowers require care until their colonies are established. Unlike cultivated plants, wildflowers haven't been bred and selected to survive in the "typical" garden. They aren't generic. Instead, they tend to be stubborn and headstrong plants with specific wants and needs. Before adopting a wildflower, study its native habitat, then try to replicate that environment as closely as possible. If the right conditions are met, the flowers will thrive.

There is a flip side to wildflower gardening. Not every wildflower is a welcome guest. There can be a fine line between nurturing an exotic wildflower and inviting an aggressive weed into your midst. Without the proper climatic controls and predators, wildflowers can run rampant, so beautiful introductions can have devastating consequences, nudging out indigenous plants that may grow less strongly. In the United States, loosestrife chokes the waterways of the Northeast, kudzu encroaches on the Southeast, honeysuckle engulfs the Midwest and leafy spurge grows roughshod in the West. Nature is a delicate balance – so be cautious. Before you plant, learn as much as you can about the personality of the plant you are inviting into your garden. A good starting point is to choose wildflowers indigenous to your region rather than dabbling in exotics from further afield. One ecosystem's heirloom can become another area's nightmare.

Miriam Rothschild, wildflower gardener

Miriam Rothschild is arguably Britain's best-known wildflower gardener, an inspiration to legions of followers. She threw away any gardening rule book years ago, and her own garden is a stunning example of a wildflower and wildlife paradise.

If you are lucky enough to visit her at her house in Northamptonshire, England, you may wonder at first if you've come to the right place. A long drive winds its way through fields full of wildflowers to a patch of woodland which hides a mysterious house, completely shrouded in vegetation.

Whatever the season, the house is alive, covered in a glorious (and planned) jumble of wild and once cultivated climbing plants, rambling from grass to sky – cultivated and wild roses and buddleias, old man's beard and rampant clematis, wisteria, ivy and other creepers, all thronging with birds and butterflies, even the occasional small mammal!

Once invited in, you find that the plants don't stop at the front door. In spring the generous dining room windowsill is filled with trays full of native wildflowers such as oxslips, primroses and lady's smock. And the overgrown grass terraces in the garden beyond are filled with native wild species – from wild garlic to bee orchids – as well as tulips, dwarf narcissi and iris. Some early introductions such as martagon lilies and bear grass mingle with the native plants.

In summer the gravel paths are lined with poppies, cornflowers, corncockles, feverfew, marigolds and flax, a mixture Miriam Rothschild has named "Farmer's Nightmare". These are resown each year, although some will also self-seed.

Once it was only the outermost terrace wall that dropped into the hayfields, but now the long grass reaches right up to the library steps; it is mown only once a year apart from the paths cut in swathes across it, leading from the house to ponds where grass snakes swim lazily across the water on sunny days, or down to the meadows where herds of rare deer graze and rear their young in peace.

Miriam Rothschild has overseen the transformation of her gardens from Edwardian showgardens full of award-winning cultivated flowers and fruit, to their present state where wildlife flourishes and nature has her way. Even the once formal glasshouses have been redeployed to nurture butterflies, wild creatures or seedlings of wild flowers – although one glasshouse is kept for the sensuous delight of strolling past heavily scented roses and jasmine. Where there were once productive vegetable plots, young plants of cowslips, primroses, violets and oxeye daisies grow in long rows like radishes, prior to being transplanted into position, or sold.

Although Miriam Rothschild turned into a wildflower gardener in response to the need to conserve our wild flora before it was too late, she also acknowledges that sentiment comes into it: "I had returned to a nostalgic but genuine delight in wildflowers, in ridge and furrow lacquered with buttercups, quaking grass and the scent of new mown hay."

The redevelopment of a natural habitat has brought numerous species of flora – as well as fauna – in from the cold. Four species of orchid have appeared in the ex-lawns, and the whole garden is a haven for butterflies and insects; dragonflies have their own special lake beyond the garden.

For all the sense of profusion or even confusion, Miriam Rothschild's wildflower plantings are planned with the precision one would expect from an acclaimed scientist. It is not just the garden which is sown with wildflowers, but whole areas of meadowland are devoted to growing the flowers for beauty, and for seed.

Most of the wildflowers sprang originally from seed collected from abandoned airfields, and that store of seed is increased each year and made available to prospective wildflower gardeners. Hay meadows contain around 120 species of wild plants, from which the seed is harvested with a combine harvester to be saved and sold or re-drilled in September or the following March. Perennial flowers are introduced near the house as seedlings, but annual flowers are sown on bare seed beds.

Miriam Rothschild wonders sometimes if nature will really take over, and if her created wilderness will bring down the house, pulling off tiles and breaking down walls. One gets the feeling she might actually approve of that scenario. Better that than the idea of a future gardener taming her wild paradise and turning it once again to manicured lawns, tennis courts and formal borders.

3

The cottage garden legacy

Many people today have a rather romantic vision of a cottage garden, a place where a mass of colours jumble happily into one another, where vegetables may mingle with the blossoms to create an idyllic rural picture. While it's true that we owe the continued existence of many of our favourite flowers to the cottage garden heritage, the picture we have today is probably quite a long way removed from how the original gardens were.

It wasn't even in the country that the very first cottage gardens appeared, but in the suburbs of the free cities of Italy and Germany in the early Middle Ages. It was here that the first free men emerged, craftsmen and tradesmen protected by their guilds and rich enough to own their own small houses. And it was in the towns that men most needed to cultivate potherbs and salads, away from the wild provisions of the countryside. However, it was the English rural cottage garden that set the style for future generations. This style has changed over centuries, developing accord-

ing to need and changing garden fashions, and in many ways it is that very changing nature of the cottage garden that characterises it. Cottage gardens have always been places where old and new have mingled happily together

In the 1340s the Black Death, or bubonic plague, struck Europe. It decimated the British population, killing a third of England's inhabitants, laying the countryside to waste and leaving manorial crops unharvested. This tragedy resulted in a new system of tenancy; suddenly, lords were forced to rent their land to tenants for income and to ensure the land was sown and harvested. As landlords came into being the cottager appeared in the English landscape and social system. Each cottage had a small garden, and so cottage gardens arrived.

The first cottage gardens were utilitarian places where food could be grown, and somewhere to keep a few chickens and a pig to add to the basic diet of cabbages (worts) and kale, onions, turnips and beans. Meat was otherwise rarely eaten, apart from an occasional

ABOVE: Yarrow *Achillea millefolium* was brought into cottage gardens early on as a wound herb

LEFT: Campanulas are traditional cottage garden favourites, grown in gardens in Northern Europe for at least 400 years

The Cottage Garden Society

One of the joys of gardening is meeting people who are interested in the same things. The Cottage Garden Society is an organisation promoting cottage gardening in all its variations – one of the first things that the Society points out to all new and prospective members is that it is not necessary to live in a country cottage to be a cottage gardener. Many of us may still be seduced by the image of the chocolate box picture of a thatched cottage with roses round the door when we think of a cottage garden, images so much loved by Victorian sentimentalist painters. But everybody can create the natural and informal style associated with the cottage garden, wherever they live.

Douglas Taylor, the Chairman of the Society, reflects that thatched cottages these days are anyway much more likely to belong to moneyed commuters than to families who have worked and lived in a village for generations, the traditional cottage gardeners. And it is more likely to be television aerials and satellite dishes that grace the walls of village dwellings than the traditional dovecotes or pigeon lofts we might have once associated with old-fashioned cottages. What's more, the cottagers who once lived without modern conveniences would probably be delighted to see such developments!

But although increased technology has brought benefits and amenities, and many places have changed almost beyond recognition, what has changed least is the style of many gardens. Some plants have come and gone, but many have lasted the test of centuries and withstood the fickle fads of fashion.

The Cottage Garden Society was formed in 1982 for the benefit of owners of small gardens who want to keep the tradition of gardening in the cottage style alive, and also to encourage an interest in old-fashioned flowers of merit and their varieties and cultivars. Members exchange seed freely, and give seed to the Society, so it is able to offer hundreds of varieties through its annual distribution scheme. Where members seek specific old-fashioned flowers, and have no luck finding them through other gardeners, the Society helps them search the specialist nurseries to locate those eagerly sought treasures.

If a would-be cottage gardener goes to a garden centre, or even a non-specialist nursery, he or she will usually be advised to choose from a fairly limited selection of hardy perennial favourites, and to follow certain rules, but Douglas Taylor reminds us that we shouldn't be nervous of trying something different, there are hundreds of garden plants suitable for cottage gardens, some offering season after season reliability, others providing a stimulating splash of colour for one season only, dying down at the end of the season to be replaced with another colourful gardening adventure the following season. Gardening evolves, there are no hard and fast rules; if you like something, give it a go, whether it is a new plant or a new technique. If it doesn't work, throw it out and start again.

While annuals have always had a place in cottage gardens, these days vegetables have largely been displaced to their own special area rather than growing happily among the flowers and herbs. Dedicated cottage gardeners seek out not just the older varieties and cultivars of flowers, but also old-fashioned varieties of vegetables – which are often much tastier than modern varieties.

Every gardener is, by definition, curious, and the more curious among us find that one of the great benefits of joining a gardening organisation is the chance to peek at other people's gardens. The Cottage Garden Society produce a list of gardens to visit, ranging from fairly substantial rural abodes with some cottage garden style herbaceous beds, to more traditional small country gardens, but also including some unexpected gardens in the middle of cities. Cottage gardens exist in countries round the world, in cities and rural outposts. Cottage gardeners can indulge their fantasies wherever their patch of ground.

rabbit poached at some risk from the landowners. There was just enough room for vegetables and salad herbs to nestle cheek by jowl, planted for harvest as needed during the growing season, with a carefully calculated surplus for storage through the winter. Beans, ground for flour as the main staple of the diet, were required in such large quantities that they generally grew in a field devoted solely to that one crop. When grains took the place of beans, they were also given a field of their own. When potatoes eventually hit the cottage garden scene, in the 17th century, they were also usually grown in a separate plot.

So cottage gardens were rooted firmly in survival, growing staple brassicas, roots, onions, leeks, and herbs for the pot. Floral refinements and adornments came after the provision of food and healing herbs. When Chaucer wrote his *Canterbury Tales* between 1386-1387, his pilgrims passed a series of humble cottages as they journeyed. And the garden that he documented was a rather rude affair. Although it was undeniably replete with vegetables and herbs, it also served other domestic functions: it was there that refuse from the house was discarded and the movable "private house" was positioned. Children played in the same area that hosted the livestock – the better-off cottagers kept a pig for the table, and chickens pecked seedlings, kept weeds at bay, controlled insects and fertilised the crops with very fresh manure. It was a simple, and not unattractive scene, but it wasn't necessarily the type of garden we would strive to recapture today.

But even early gardens had some ornamental features. During the Middle Ages monks were largely responsible for healthcare, providing herbal medicines to those that visited them, and even making calls to sick villagers. Some of their knowledge about suitable plants and cultivation techniques seeped down to the country people, as well as a few of their more ornamental plants.

By the 14th century some cottage gardens probably boasted Madonna lilies and other flowers gleaned from monastic and manorial gardens, and wildflowers useful as herbs were planted in the earliest gardens. Violets and primroses were pretty as well as useful herbs; periwinkles and cowslips were common early on, and as early as the 15th century most of the humblest gardens already had a scented rose or two, such as *R. gallica* or *R. alba*.

Gradually, more and more flowers that were beautiful as well as good for some purpose or other slipped into the beds. Even if they weren't actually "essential", some excuse was found for inviting ornamentals into the cottage yard. Given a little ingenuity, an application could be found for everything. By the 1500s, many native plants came from wood or field into the cottage garden, for example yarrow was used to reduce a fever, Lady's mantle to stop bleeding, monkshood *Aconitum anglicum*, bellflowers and columbine were used for sore throats and borage was taken to dispel melancholy. Pennyroyal was grown for flavouring water, germander for cough syrup, tansy and wormwood, betony and mullein were all among the prototypical cottage flowers. Cranesbill, foxglove, centaury and campions all appeared, interplanted with the vegetables, giving the cottage garden the informality that served as its hallmark throughout the ages.

During the Elizabethan age, the second half of the 16th century, there was a comparative improvement in the poor rural dweller's lot. Living conditions improved throughout society, and people began to take more of an interest in the way things looked. Wealthy people invested heavily in their houses and gardens and elements of the new styles filtered down to the humblest gardens. Cottage gardens began to be a little more ordered. Many had a selection of fruit trees and ornamental flowers as well as the herbs and vegetables that already made the cottage garden their home. Increasing numbers of

Believed to date from the 1700s, *Aquilegia vulgaris* 'Nora Barlow" is still available, and tends to come true from seed

Commonly called "bachelor's buttons", cornflowers, *Centaurea cyanus,* have graced cottage gardens and arable fields for centuries

flowering plants from other countries entered the scene. Lavender and clove carnations arrived from southern Europe, fritillaries came from Turkey, gladioli from the Mediterranean, lychnis was imported from Russia, the daylily arrived from China and jasmine ventured over from the Himalayas. When they first arrived, those plants were certainly not the property of the peasants but cultivated by the nobility in grander gardens. However, cuttings were easily snipped by garden boys and seed was simply collected by servants. Once exotic, these flowers became as much a part of the folk culture as the native wildflowers that preceded them.

Jasmines, clematis and (of great importance later on) the scarlet runner bean could all be found growing in cottage gardens by the end of the 16th century, along with auriculas from Flanders, Turk's cap lilies from Asia as well as wallflowers, stocks, tulips, narcissus and hyacinths. These joined the corn marigolds, sweet briar, honeysuckle, and other old regulars that originally came in from the wild. All became part of the melting pot that was the cottage garden – although the scene was not necessarily so romantic as the image conjured up by these attractive flowering plants.

As erstwhile rarities became common they were banished from the great gardens by new introductions, and cottage gardens came to pre-serve these old plants. While some of our favourite flowers had exotic beginnings and were maintained in grand gardens for centuries, we owe much of our interesting floral legacy to the enthusiasms of working class gardener. We can thank them particularly for the "florists flowers" (*see page 73*): anemones, auriculas, pinks, hyacinths, polyanthus and tulips, as well as ranunculas and shrub roses. The cottage gar-den took plants as they were provided, and hung on to them if they were pleasing. In the cottage garden, today's novelties have always sat comfortably beside yesterday's floral treasures.

The first cottage gardens were not just growing vegetables and flowers; fruit was important from the start when most gardens had an apple tree or a pear, and plums and cherries were com-mon along with some native berries.

In the 16th century many different kinds of fruit came to be grown quite widely: vines, peaches and strawberries were common in even humble gardens, probably taken from old monastic gar-dens after the dissolution of the monas-teries in 1536.

Gooseberries were grown in cottage gardens since the earliest days, but they gained increased popularity from the 16th century, and by the 19th century there were over 2,000 varieties avail-able. Few still exist.

COTTAGE GARDEN ELEMENTS

Cottage gardens all shared one universal trait. By necessity, they were all surrounded by a hedge or fence of one sort or another. After all, roaming livestock had to be kept at bay and the household pig and chickens had to be constrained. To prevent the inroads of nibbling passersby, the cottage garden fence was necessarily sturdy and well-maintained, and hedges were often encouraged to reach barricade proportions.

The hedge or fence defined and protected the outer boundaries of a cottage garden, within which the garden was laid out in the simple design of straight rectangular beds, sometimes raised but more often laid simply side by side with flowers scattered between the brief rows of herbs and food crops, with straight brick or stone paths dividing beds. Although the cottage garden appeared to be a confusion of cabbages and cornflowers, larkspur and lettuces when in full swing, the sense of profusion was created by the plants rather than the design.

If there was a formal element to the cottage garden, it surfaced in the living sculptures of meticulously clipped topiary, often featuring birds such as peacocks, or even castellations. Cottage gardeners seemed to have an abiding fascination with topiary for centuries, an art borrowed from the gardens of the great estates – often brought back by undergardeners – and embraced wholeheartedly. The hedge had to be kept within bounds, and it was more interesting and challenging, as well as making an individual statement, to clip it into some fanciful shape. Shrubs were also sometimes sheared to shape – apparently rosemary, grown for medicinal, culinary and housecleaning purposes, was frequently clipped into whimsical shapes in the 16th century, but this could only be accomplished by the woman of the house, while hedges were strictly the man's territory.

Vines were usually encouraged to clamber up whatever was at hand. The chicken coop and outhouse provided vertical walls for some, while others were supported up columns or wigwams of hazel sticks. Apart from the space-saving advantage of vertically growing productive plants, fragrant vines served important functions in the yard where the family most often congregated in summer. Their scent, beautiful in its own right, also conveniently masked the smells of the privy, and vines often clambered around its walls. Hop vines became a common character in latter day cottage gardens, but they were absent in early ones – hops were forbidden in Britain by Henry VI and didn't appear in cottage gardens much before the 18th century.

Arbours were never a feature of the poorest gardens, but became popular in yeomen's gardens from the 15th century onward, providing a foothold for vines and welcome shade under which to perform some of the household tasks such as scrubbing the laundry or shelling the beans. Ironically, arbours have become one of the most popular features of later, retrospective cottage gardens, surviving into modern times along with the old-fashioned climbers they nurtured.

Old-fashioned flowers often seemed unkempt because of their dimensions. Most cottage garden plants used to be tall and lanky. If things tumbled one into the next, it was partly because they all bore long stems balancing a few blossoms on top before breeders took them in hand in the 19th century and evened out the ratio. Thereafter the cottage garden was not easy to recreate. Tidy new annuals just don't do the trick. Long stems, subtle colours, and plants with a long flowering season created the look.

Certain plants have always worked well within the cottage garden venue. They have to be capable of enduring without complaint all the changes in climate typical of an average year as well as an occasional severe season. And they

LEFT TO RIGHT: Cottage garden favourites: Larkspur *Consolida ambigua* and lupins *Lupinus perennis*

TOP RIGHT: Lemon daylilies *Hemerocallis* BELOW: Morning glory *Ipomoea tricolor*

tend to be noteworthy – little nondescript plants that can't compete favourably with their neighbours have rarely been introduced, nor botanical bullies other than those early wildflowers originally invited in for medicinal purposes. By the 18th century most of what we consider to be common cottage garden flowers had arrived. Spired bloomers such as foxgloves, larkspur, aconites, hyacinths and lupins were prevalent. Scabious, alliums, stocks, wallflowers, anemones and ranunculas grew alongside peonies and hollyhocks. Fragrance was especially coveted and could be found in pinks, roses, primroses, daffodils, lavender and nepeta. Any plant was invited to stay if it had a cheerful presence.

One important function of a cottage garden, in today's terms, is as a repository of old-fashioned flowers and knowledge. Some of these gardens are gene pools preserving genetic information that would otherwise be lost. There are stories of, for example, a particular strain of stocks preserved in the cottage gardens of a small Scottish neighborhood for 350 years. And of a particular nutmeg clove pink preserved in one garden since 1652.

Curiously, some of the plants we consider cottage garden mainstays are relatively recent: bleeding hearts *Dicentra*, for example, were introduced only a century ago. The bearded iris so popular today are 20th century developments. No cottage garden would be complete without lupins, but these plants changed their character completely earlier this century; early cottage gardeners would scarcely recognise today's strong multicoloured plants. The first of the hybrid delphiniums which are so widely grown today were not bred until the 19th century. Although violets have been grown in cottage gardens for many centuries, the ubiquitous garden pansy *Viola* x *wittrockiana* is another comparatively recent creation. Throughout their history, cottage gardens have never been static affairs.

COTTAGE GARDENS REVISITED

The cottage garden landscape remained the province of peasants, small farmers, artisans and and tradespeople for centuries. Moneyed gardeners kept their landscapes clipped and current with the trends. The slightly scruffy, rather dirty behind the ears cottage garden seemed inferior to people who had the sophistication to follow fashion and keep abreast of the newest and latest foreign introductions.

By the end of the 18th century things were changing. Rural life was very hard for poor people with a vast gap between rich and poor, but the wealthy increasingly began to want to change the landscape to create some sort of rural idyll. Suddenly, people who commanded many hundred acres and could afford the salaries of several full time gardeners to clip formal plantings, installed little thatched cottages somewhere in their domain and surrounded those quaint little cottages with chocolate-box gardens. They began to romanticise the simple life and model villages were built to house some workers (actually built not from philanthropic ideals but through the need to sanitise the picture of the countryside.) The model housing was in fact a vast improvement for most new tenants.

This was a time when sentimentality was the predominant emotion. People had an image – through pictures and magazines – of happy and healthy clean and shining rosy-faced countryfolk; the harsher realities of rural life were obscured. The romanticism of the cottage garden appealed to a class that certainly need not dwell in a humble cottage. By the end of the late 19th century the rural realm was fashionable. Suddenly, cottage gardens were in the forefront of fashion, they became models for fashionable planting and the traditional plants they nurtured were sought after and given a hero's welcome by gardeners who could afford to buy whatever they wanted.

Prominent horticultural commentators, notably William Robinson (1838-1935) and Gertrude Jekyll (1843-1932), were particularly forceful in their praise of cottage gardens. This was a time of divided gardening, with on the one hand a desire for a return to rurality, and on the other an urge to complete gardening excess. The new fashion for carpet bedding meant that wealthy garden owners encouraged incredibly wasteful planting schemes of labour intensive annual exotics, raised by their thousands in heated glasshouses, planted out by armies of cheap labour and pulled out when their moment of splendour was passed to be replanted with a different colour, later-flowering annual, and so on through the season. Robinson and Jekyll recognised beauty in the old-fashioned cottage garden with its permanence and waves of seasonal glory. They sought to recapture that mood.

William Robinson is sometimes called the prophet of natural gardening. Much of what he advised reflected the feelings of contemporary artists and thinkers such as those involved in the Arts and Crafts movement in England, a reaction against Victorian mass production and industrialisation. Robinson wrote venomously about annual bedding schemes, calling them "the ugliest gardens ever made", and lovingly about the cottage style.

Robinson only allowed foreign plants into the garden if they behaved like natives. He advocated planting only hardy plants, and advised gardeners to understand how and where plants grow in the wild. They should then be placed in the garden next to neighbours which liked the same kind of environment, and each group should be allowed to spread naturally to form generous natural looking swathes of planting. He was really the first advocate of ecological gardening. He gradually transformed his own large garden over 50 years into an ideal cottage-style garden, his combinations of plants managing to retain the simplicity at the heart of

William Robinson was a gardener and a journalist. In 1871 he founded a magazine called The Garden, but probably his most influential work was his book The English Flower Garden, first published in 1883.

His influence on plants and gardens remains important today; most herbaceous borders refer – albeit sometimes unconsciously – to some of Robinson's ideas. His love of cottage garden planting was reflected in his own garden at Gravetye Manor, in Sussex, England. This garden has been faithfully restored and is open to visitors (see page 183). Robinson's definition of a cottage garden serves just as well today as when he wrote it over a century ago:

"Cottage gardeners are good to their plots and in the course of years they make them fertile; and the shelter of the little house and hedge favours the flowers. But there is something more, and it is the absence of any pretentious 'plan', which lets the flowers tell their story to the heart."

Fences provide vertical climbing space for scented jasmine *Jasminum officinale,* or a backdrop to the spindly *Verbena bonariensis*

the tradition. He also retained a respect and love of growing good food to eat, encouraging fruit and vegetables into every garden, just as in the first cottage gardens.

Gertrude Jekyll was especially keen on reviving a lifestyle that she saw as endangered, but her approach was slightly different from Robinson's. She was a painter before she was a gardener and saw everything through an artist's eye. She was driven around the countryside, stopping at cottage gardens to chat with the cottagers and extract their secrets. She noted the resident flora and requested cuttings or seeds if the plant happened to strike her fancy. She railed against pelargoniums, she decried strident colours and suggested a billowing garden much simpler than the currently fashionable fancy annual borders. She transformed formal landscapes into places where lady's mantle and catmint spilled beyond the edges of the borders. She showed how herbaceous plants could provide as pleasing seasonal displays as annuals, designing spring gardens, summer gardens and autumn gardens that were glorious during their moment and then were clipped severely back to come again the following year.

Miss Jekyll's gardens were characterised by thoughtful planting in stunning colour combinations. They were enormously influential although their artistry was derived rather than copied from cottage garden style. These neo-cottage gardens were scrubbed-up, pared-down versions of the original, but with many similar elements. Most notably, this time around, the vegetables were all but nosed out in favour of flowers.

Meanwhile, the 19th century saw the great development of many traditional flowers at the hands of hybridisers. Campanulas, larkspur, roses, poppies, peonies, cosmos, cleome, dianthus were all *de rigueur*. New colours were created, and new growth habits were encouraged, making the new cottage garden a cleaner affair that it ever dreamed of being when it was born in the 1300s.

The romanticised cottage garden employed and elaborated on many of the same structures as its predecessors. A bee skep had been utilitarian in gardens since the earliest medieval examples when honey was an important sweetener; it was suddenly transformed to provide a quaint focal point. Wellheads were fancified as they had never been before, and the yeoman's arbour metamorphosed into the gazebo or – even more elaborately – the summerhouse. Dovecotes became fashionable garden features, with bird houses for common and exotic fowl. Peacocks could sometimes be found strutting the cottage paths as well as other rare birds of every feather. Containers, previously purely functional to coddle tender valuables such as precious calceolarias and dahlias, became widespread and increasingly decorative. Other ornamental elements filtered in. Sundials and rustic furniture of all descriptions were added as focal points or resting areas in the midst of a place where profusion demanded a respite. Fountains, statues and other features trickled in from more formal gardens. The cottage garden had strayed from its original roots, but the forum that had nurtured the earliest flowers was preserved.

During the last 50 years society has changed more drastically than in the previous five hundred. Gardening has become primarily a leisure pursuit rather than the matter of survival which necessitated the development of the earliest cottage gardens. Flowers can be bought easily at a multitude of garden centres and nurseries, even at garages and corner shops, so many people don't see the need to hang on to what we've got, to preserve the gardening culture and plants of the past. But the simple beauty of traditional cottage garden plants is timeless. They have stood the test of centuries and have been used in different ways through history; they are reliable, easy to grow, and tried-and-tested.

AMERICAN COTTAGE GARDENS

Just as the British working class had simple gardens, the earliest colonial gardens in America were also hardworking affairs. The modern interpretation of a proper Pilgrim garden is a series of neatly clipped, boxwood-edged herb beds. However, that landscape was more accurately the garden of a wealthy landowner. At first, early settlers on the northeast coast of America tended the same sort of cottage gardens as they had in Britain; the early American cottage gardeners had all the billowing blossoms and well-manured cabbages that they had previously cultivated in their homeland.

The mood of the American cottage garden was the same utilitarian affair as its European predecessors, but the inventory was slightly different. John Josselyn chronicled his successes and failures with Old World plants in his 1672 treatise, *New England's Rarities Discovered*. He enjoyed success with spearmint, feverfew, santolina, pennyroyal, ground ivy, house leek, hollyhocks, comfrey, coriander, dill, anise, asparagus, sorrel, sweet briar, English roses, tansy and peppermint. However, despite his most concerted efforts, celandine grew slowly, bloodwort sorrily, and fennel had to be taken up and kept in a warm cellar for winter. Furthermore, southernwood was no plant for North America, nor rosemary, nor bay. Rue would hardly grow.

The Pilgrims weren't as eager to welcome American wildflowers into their gardens as their British ancestors had been to adopt the native flora into the cultivated landscape. With a vast wilderness to tame and a relatively meagre plot under cultivation, they stuck fairly faithfully to fillers that were considered garden plants.

The cottage garden didn't become popular once again in America when the style was revived in Britain. Perhaps it could be blamed on the fact that Americans had larger tracts of land at their disposal, or perhaps the reason lay

in the fact that suburban homes rarely featured fences. Americans preferred a wide open vista with a few foundation shrubs hugging the ankles of their houses. They were unlikely to obscure the view of their proud abode with a crowd of flowers between the front door and the drive. Furthermore, the focus of activities was towards the backyard which afforded privacy in lieu of a fence.

One of North America's great gardeners was Thomas Jefferson (1743-1826). He loved flowers and experimented with many different plants including vegetables and crops in his large kitchen garden and neighbouring farms. The Thomas Jefferson Center for Historic Plants at Monticello, Virginia, now grows plants that were known to have been grown by Jefferson and his contemporaries. Many of these are what we might consider old-fashioned cottage garden favourites, such as old species and cultivars of hollyhocks, flowering tobacco and French mallow and cockscomb, as well as Jefferson's wine-red species snapdragon, his scarlet pentapetes *Pentapetes phoenicia*, and the original single-flowering Mexican zinnia species *Zinnia pauciflora*.

For many reasons, the closely snuggled cottage scene was not the American aesthetic, but quite suddenly there is a renewed interest in old-fashioned gardens in America, although these are often generically labelled as "romantic gardens". These latter day landscapes have the same profusion, informality and plant palette that predominated the cottage landscapes of long ago.

Although few contemporary American gardeners have ploughed up their front lawns to plant delphiniums, foxglove, salvias and Lady's mantle, traditional plants are becoming popular once again. Not only are the new cottage gardens of interest from a design perspective, they also serve to sharpen public awareness of our floral heritage when many flowers are in serious danger of being lost.

Cosmos was greatly developed in the early 20th century, producing forms such as this 'Seashells'

Old-fashioned outhouse hollyhocks *Alcea rosea* have been grown in cottage gardens for centuries

An English cottage garden in America

Close your eyes and imagine a cottage garden, and you'll probably conjure up a vision not far removed from the voluptuous landscape that wraps around Tasha Tudor's Corgi Cottage in northern New England. There, a complex labyrinth of paths so slender that you must walk single file (and often snag your hem nevertheless) wind up a breakneck hill. There, chimney bellflowers, 17th century dianthus, poppies that came from Tasha's Scottish nanny and roses that remain nameless, but have travelled with Tasha from home to home throughout her long life, surround a cottage in a cloud of blossoms during New England's brief but dramatic growing season.

The gardens look back to another era, as does the cottage. Corgi Cottage was built less than thirty years ago, but the house was constructed to look as if it had been in place for two hundred years or more. Vines climb up arbours curved over the pathways, climbers encase little thickets hiding a table and chairs where tea is served when Tasha takes the time to carry the Canton china gingerly down the hill.

The walls of the house are covered in rambling plants which snare your curls as you wander by beds dense with poet's narcissus, tulips, violas, forget-me-nots, crown imperials, hollyhocks, fragrant iris and two-tone sweet peas. The season is short, so even the porch is strewn with potted bulbs and lilies forced to open long before those grown in open ground. A children's illustrator by profession and inclination, Tasha's flowers serve a practical function – acting as models for her work. But really, that's just an excuse. The profusion of flowers has been amassed because Tasha is first and foremost a collector. She collects old garden tools, rickety wheelbarrows, Belgian pots by the stackload, lustreware, crockery and handwoven baskets. Inside the cottage, vintage clothing crowds her attic, antique textiles fill the drawers. Tasha accumulates profusion in every area of her life.

And she collects plants with the same compulsion that drives her to acquire all things old and wonderful. So it's no surprise that scarcely a square foot around Corgi Cottage is left unplanted. But it's not a hodgepodge. There are no strident shades, all the melodious colours harmonise, right through the seasons. You can walk out of her back door at any time between May and September to find a splendid display spread before you. It's all seamlessly executed. Yet, Tasha says: "I never designed the garden," she insists, "it just grew like Topsy."

Tasha admits that the stone walls were drawn out on paper. "And if I had those walls built today, I wouldn't let Mr. Herrick waiver from my plan one inch," she'll proclaim. "I told him to bend the wall inward with pockets to tuck in pinks and whatnot. Instead, he built her straight and now she's beginning to lean out. I wouldn't let it happen today, I can promise you. I've grown savage in my old age."

As for the plantings, they have increased over the years, by whim and will. Some seeded themselves without compunction. Others were invited to increase, but not necessarily through great expenditure. Whenever Tasha buys plants, she purchases them in quantities of three, which might lead you to believe that some guidelines are being followed. But there's no master plan. "I buy three and put each in a different situation. I watch, I see if one thrives, and then I move the others to that same sort of place."

When Tasha feels as though she's failing with a plant, she takes immediate action. Books are pulled off the shelf and consulted, professors at northern universities are called upon, letters are written to experts in the field. Nothing is planted and then forgotten. Tasha is a model steward. Corgi Cottage might not have a master plan, but a great deal of caring and nurturing is invested in each flowerbed.

MODERN COTTAGE GARDENS

Throughout history the wealthy have always been able to buy their gardeners straight from the designer, so-to-speak. You can't imagine the early European aristocracy designing or supervising the planting of hundreds of formal avenues in intricately laid out arrangements. I don't suppose there was a single Elizabethan noblemen who designed and planted his own elaborate knot garden, and so on through the ages. Nowadays it is not only the seriously wealthy who have their gardens provided in a finished form, but people from all classes and with varying amounts of money. Gardens have alweays been symbols of status and taste for certain groups of people, and there have always been people willing to pay to adopt someone else's style. This is the exact opposite of cottage gardening.

The great thing about cottage gardens is that they are relaxed places, they develop with you. And they are not really places that are too influenced by the ideas of others. While Gertrude Jekyll and her ilk were undeniably great gardeners, while modern garden designers also have a lot of important points to make about planting, their plans can never capture the real essence of cottage gardening: cottage gardens are each unique to their particular gardener, they don't spring up overnight but take time, developing with the gardener more than according to current fads and fashions. The best cottage gardens have developed over decades or lifetimes.

So cottage gardens embody what is the real joy of gardening – experimenting. If something works it stays, and if you don't like it after a season or two you can simply take it out, move it or pass it on to somebody else. You make mistakes or errors of judgment, and change them; the early cottage gardeners weren't influenced by other people's style decisions, modern gardeners don't need to be either.

If many of the modern plants had been around, earlier gardeners would probably have leapt at the chance to use them, but there is something very special about the traditional cottage garden plants; they have a certain simplicity and beauty about them that is hard to define but which you appreciate when you grow them. And the most important thing about them is that they are all easy to grow. When early cottage gardeners were planting their gardens, they didn't have time to worry about how their plants were faring, they were too busy trying to survive; of course they looked after them, ensuring the soil was fertile and pests, if any, were checked, but there was little mollycoddling. If something didn't thrive, it couldn't stay.

Most of the old favourites can be grown by simple division or from seed; most of them are extremely hardy and reliable; most of them spread happily without too much human intervention. When gardeners first invited plants in from the wild they would have seen how they grew in their natural habitat and copied the conditions as closely as possible. When they were given plants by friends and neighbours they would learn the plant's habits with the gift, and how to propagate it. They didn't need greenhouses and fancy gadgets, just soil. So many of our best-loved flowers are extremely easy to grow and look after. Plants wouldn't have survived for so long if they were tricky as anyone will get disheartened if they fail continuously at propagating them or growing them. Most old-fashioned flowers are suitable for anyone to grow, whether they have a tiny and unsophisticated plot or rather a grand garden, whether they are experienced or amateur gardeners.

The cottage garden has always proved a good home to old-fashioned flowers. But they can be grown anywhere – in a front cottage garden, in your backyard, on a balcony, or in a container. Just grow them and enjoy them.

4

Flowers gained and lost

The original cottage gardeners had no reason to search far or spend their hard-earned wages on blossoms to uplift their gardens. Flowers – and vegetables – were passed along freely from one gardener to the next, shared from cottage to cottage. There wasn't a huge working repertoire, and it was handed on. Cottage gardens owed their heart and soul to a few tried-and-tested favourites; by the 17th century inveterate performers such as columbines, clove pinks, marigolds, borage, lavender, violets, dog roses, honeysuckle, lilies and iris could be found in most cottage gardens. Some of these plants would first have been brought in from the wild, others would have gradually arrived from cultivation, sometimes acquired from monasteries or from undergardeners on big estates.

Sophisticated gardeners have always accused the commonly planted flowers of being botanical clichés, and refused to accommodate them in their fashionable gardens for many centuries. They relied on novelties from abroad, brought home by collectors and gradually disseminated among a limited gardening class. Old-fashioned flowers were not much sought after commodities until recently.

The seed and nursery business grew up long after the birth and blossoming of cottage gardens, coinciding with British colonial expansion and widening trade routes. The early nurserymen-gardeners were likely to be gentlemen indulging (albeit extremely professionally) in a part-time occupation. By the 17th century a number of nurserymen collectors were specialising in particular flowers. John Rea, for example was growing over 200 named varieties of tulips in his English garden by 1650, but these were certainly not for sale to all and sundry. Although several tree nurseries had been established in Europe for at least 150 years, supplying specimen and woodland trees for the gardens and orchards of aristocrats and monarchs, trade in flowers was rare before the 1700s. The horticultural trade was primarily developed to feed wealthier gardeners' desires for novelties.

ABOVE: Shirley poppies *Papaver rhoeas* were first selected and developed by the Reverend William Wilks in 1880

LEFT: Clematis 'Belle de Woking' is a hybrid developed at George Jackman's famous 19th century English clematis nursery

Supplying historic plants

If you want to find a specific plant to fit a historic planting scheme, a particularly fragrant pink, or a rare campanula, a visit to Derek and Judy Tolman's Buckinghamshire nursery is a rewarding one.

The Tolmans' nursery grew out of the desire to find old-fashioned plants for their own garden. In the 1980s they moved into an ancient cottage and decided they wanted to create a garden to match. But they found it was not easy to track down the sort of plants they wanted. Cottage garden plants weren't fashionable then, and old-fashioned varieties were definitely considered marginal; nurseries at that time were concentrating on bedding plants or shrubs.

The quest for interesting plants gradually took the Tolmans over. They became increasingly fascinated by the history of plants, where they came from, what they had first been called, when they were first grown in Britain, and where they could be obtained.

Even when they came across the plants they wanted it was often difficult to purchase more than one or two examples. Reasoning that they were probably not the only people interested in finding fitting plants for old gardens, Derek and Judy decided to remedy this situation by changing direction away from their previous occupations in commerce and law into plants, propagating what they found to increase the stock available to would-be historic gardeners.

So Bernwode Nursery was created, where Derek and Judy produce plants that they like. And other people seem to like them too. They provide a mail order service as well as welcoming visitors to the nursery, and both sides of the business are thriving.

Bernwode Nursery is the first point of call for garden conservationists and designers whenever major restoration projects are underway. It is a nursery with a purpose, but it is not only for specialists. This is first and foremost a nursery run by and for enthusiasts.

All plant catalogues make interesting reading to gardeners, even the armchair sort, but Bernwode Plants' catalogue is one of those rare treats, a literary as well as horticultural feast. Plants come alive on the page, offering mystery and irresistible promise: 'Angelica Archangelica: Angelica, Holy Ghost. Called Angelica because an angel was said to have revealed its use in fighting the plague. It was also used to ward off witches and hung in cattle sheds to prevent diseases which were thought to be spread by elves. Grown since the early sixteenth century, chiefly for culinary purposes, though it also makes a very stately plant. The young shoots are delicious when candied and used in cakes and puddings. Biennial, but perennial if the flower heads are removed before seeding. 6 feet. Grows in sun or shade.'

Derek Tolman is a plantsman with a fascination for plant history, and a desire to spread the word. He has entered data on his computer to compile lists of plants known to be grown in England at specific dates, and he is happy to give those lists to customers. You can ask for plants grown before 1700, for example, and Derek will provide a dozen or so pages of accurate names and dates. Or a customer can ask for very precise details, perhaps requesting a purple flower that will flourish in shade, reach no more than 18 inches (40cm) and is known to have been cultivated in English gardens before 1840: Derek will press a few buttons and come up with a selection of answers.

Nothing is bought in, all plants are home grown in containers, and plants in the sales area are clearly labelled and arranged in alphabetical order with symbols for sun, shade and, where relevant, if the plant is poisonous. Moreover, the Tolman's try to use organic methods, resembling the conditions in which many of the early flowers would originally have grown.

If its fragrance you're seeking, visit the nursery in June when many of the nursery's old pinks are flowering, assailing the nostrils. Few people could resist the temptation to purchase one or more of the 100 or so cultivars and varieties on offer. Many of them have the additional pull of evocative names such as 'Caesar's Mantle', or the 'Bloody pink'; 'Fenbow's Nutmeg Clove' – believed to date from the 14th century; 'Frank's Frilly', and 'Pheasant's Ear'. Here you can find not only the old double white 'Mrs Sinkins', but also a pink sport, along with numerous other rarities.

But Bernwode Nursery can be a dangerous place, not only because of plants marked with the skull and crossbow symbol such as the Tolmans' home-bred Aconitum wilsonii 'The Grim Reaper', but because it is almost impossible for any gardener to escape without purchasing far more plants than originally intended!

One of the first examples of selling flowering plants was recorded in 1667, when George Ricketts, nurseryman of Hoxton, near London, sent a list of fruit trees for sale to Sir Thomas Hanmer. The list included 23 varieties of gilliflowers (*Dianthus*). In 1670 Hanmer's journals mentioned also receiving anemones and auricula primroses from George Ricketts. While the earliest Botanic Gardens were established in Pisa and Padua, followed by Paris, the most famous early nurseries were situated in London. One of the best-known was "the great Nursery between Spittle-fields and White-chappel" established in 1643 by Captain Leonard Gurle who later became King Charles II's royal gardener. Gurle sold trees but he was also one of the first to sell flower seeds. The Brompton Park Nursery was another large venture; at its peak in the early 1700s, it covered 100 acres of central London, employed 20 men (and two women) and kept a stock of 40,000 plants.

The earliest surviving plant list comes not from England but from the Parisian nurseryman René Morin in 1621, and already included a mention of pelargoniums, brought from their native Cape of Good Hope to Holland but first cultivated successfully by Morin. But the first giant step in the seed selling direction came in 1677 when William Lucas, a member of the London Society of Florists, published the first plant list truly dedicated to seed retailing. Operating at The Naked Boy, he offered a comprehensive list of seeds, bulbs and roots of salads, herbs, trees and flowers. Snapdragons, French honeysuckle, scabious, larkspur, columbines, sweet sultan, lychnis, impatiens, nasturtium, Canterbury bells, foxgloves, amaranths, aconites, convolvulus, African and French marigolds, poppies, wallflowers and gilliflowers were on his seed list, as well as roots and bulbs of ranunculus, anemones, crocus, cyclamen and lilies, fritillaries, crown imperials (yellow, double and single) jasmines, paeonies

During the 17th and 18th centuries, a florist was not a flower seller, as today, but a specialist breeder and grower. The first florists were rich country gentlemen with estates, often buying their original stocks from abroad.

When numbers of new plants began to arrive in Britain from America and elsewhere during the 1700s, some florists lost interest in their role and became collectors, a few became professional nurserymen.

Then a new race of florists arose from the working class; these florists were poor men, factory workers, petty tradesmen, artisans and miners who developed an astonishing range of those flowers often referred to as "florists flowers": tulips, primroses, ranunculus, auriculas, polyanthus, pinks, hyacinths and carnations.

In the 19th century these florists developed many beautiful cultivars. Sadly few remain available today but those that still exist are eagerly sought after by collectors.

Honeysuckle *Lonicera periclymenum* is a temptingly fragrant climber, tolerant of most climates and soil conditions

(black, red, purple and striped), hellebores, and double, striped and plain auricula primroses. Over 140 flowers were offered, with herbs sold under a different category. The list provides a sketch of popular early flowers.

Obviously, the climate was favourable, because other merchants followed Lucas' lead. The same list was published in 1688 in the appendix of J. Woolridge's book, *Systema horti-culturae*, and attributed to three different London merchants, namely Edward Fuller who succeeded Lucas as the proprietor of The Naked Boy, Theophilus Stacy at The Rose and Crown, and Charles Blackwell of The King's Head. By 1760, the number of nurseries selling seeds, plants and trees had swelled to approximately 100 firms operating in Britain.

London was the centre of British trade, but the early merchants were not solely dependent on domestic customers. This was an expansionary period for the United Kingdom and the colonies proved an eager audience. In particular, pioneers in the newly settled wilderness of America were keen on establishing a home-away-from-home and receiving the necessary seeds of their former flowering favourites to realise that goal.

Trade with North America was established early on, initiated in 1631 by John Winthrop, Jr, son of the Governor of the colony of Massachusetts. He applied to Robert Hill, grocer of a shop called The Three Angels in London's Lombard Street, for a supply of garden seeds which he took with him to America. These included a few recent introductions but the bulk were European natives, including columbines, clary sage, marigolds, hollyhocks, monkshood, poppies, sweet rocket, stock-gilliflowers *Matthiola incana*, tansy and wallflowers, as well as some favourite roses. There was nothing too exotic to begin with as the early colonials' lives were too busy for too much pleasure gardening. But it was the start of a

healthy exchange between the two continents. The colonists sought seeds of favourite plants unavailable in the New World, and many also struggled to remain abreast of the latest introductions from newly explored lands. Novelties were arriving in Europe at a brisk pace from explorations funded by wealthy aristocrats and enterprising nurserymen. Those plants were then duly distributed. As early as 1655 Dutch settlers in New Holland and New Amsterdam were growing fine tulips, crown imperials and several kinds of lilies as well as old favourites such as violets, anemones, and red and white roses.

The relationship worked both ways; distinguished London-based nurserymen such as James Lee and Conrad Loddiges fell over each other to offer European clients rarities obtained from the New World. But North America was not the only destination for plant hunters, nor was it the only country to feed the hunger for new plants. A vigorous market clamoured for anything foreign and novel. In the latter quarter of the 1700s, James Lee's nursery alone introduced some 135 exotics from Siberia, South Africa, Chile, Madeira, China, Australia, Mexico, Guinea and the West Indies, in addition to the plants that came from North America. Many of the latter were culled from North America's vast native flora, much greater than that in Europe, and became essential perennials for gardens great and small.

Traditional plants from one continent became fixtures in gardens farther afield, and trading in seeds and plants was a vigorous business. By 1840, over 150 nurserymen were engaged in brisk business in Britain, with 30 principal firms plus a number of smaller ones in London, the rest scattered throughout England. Individual nurserymen played an important role in the development of gardening,

North Americans were relatively slow to adopt the business of selling plants. John

One of the most influential nurserymen before 1800 was Conrad Loddiges, a German with a nursery in Hackney, London. His first catalogue in 1777 was produced in three languages, English, German and Latin, showing the importance of the continental as well as the British markets. At that time the nursery was best known for the American plants sent by John Bartram's son, William, who had continued collecting plants after his father's death.

Horticulture was clearly big business in this expansionary period, and Loddiges' 1826 catalogue described 8,000 different species for sale, including 67 of oak, 29 of birch, 91 of thorns, 180 of willow and 1,549 different roses. Approximately 2,000 imported plants could be purchased only through his nursery.

Moreover, the nursery arboretum covered more than seven acres (3 hectares) and was laid out like a scroll with species beginning with the letter A at the outer circumference and the letter Z (Zizyphus) in the centre.

Bartram opened his collection of botanical novelties to fellow Philadelphians in 1728, followed two years later by Robert Prince who established the Linnaean Botanical Garden in Flushing, New York in 1730. Initially, those establishments were devoted strictly to science, educating the public and showing off the remarkable rarities these two plant hunters had amassed. You could come and admire, but you couldn't purchase. Later, Robert Prince's grandson (William Prince II, 1766-1842) finally saw an audience for his plants and catered to public demand by propagating and selling stock from his collection. It was a step in a fruitful direction, but several years passed before a definitive trade in plants was attempted.

In 1784, David Landreth, a recent immigrant to Philadelphia from Britain, was the first North American to open a shop devoted to selling horticultural goods. He subsequently welcomed his sons into the business and added 30 acres (75 hectares) of land to supply the demand for his seed. Landreth featured some old faithfuls, but he was most proud of his inventory of exotics such as camellias, rhododendrons, hyacinth, citrus, bananas and the bird of Paradise *Strelitzia reginae*. Other Philadelphians opened similar botanical establishments, notably Bernard M'Mahon in 1800. In 1802, Grant Thorburn introduced the trend into New York City, soon specialising in pelargoniums which became so popular that they were almost a symbol of the new country, with settlers crossing the continent with pelargoniums on their covered wagons and later on their windowsills.

Most popular plants were novelties at first, buyers scrambling to purchase them and remain one step ahead of their neighbours. If the plant was worthy, it spread widely via seedsellers, plant businesses andother gardeners. Eventually, the novelty wore thin. For a while it was commonplace, then replaced by something more exciting. What is old today was once new.

Viola tricolor, also known as heartsease, was grown by the Elizabethans

Grandpa Ott's morning glory inspired the foundation of Seed Savers Exchange and the Flower and Herb Exchange

FLOWERS OF YESTERDAY

Over the centuries there have been definite trends in preferred flower forms. The definition of how the perfect flower should appear has changed with time. Even the universally accepted symbol of beauty, the rose, has changed dramatically in appearance through centuries of selection and breeding.

Varieties offered in 19th century catalogues often boasted different attributes from today's flowers. One of the most dramatic changes is the gradual decrease in height. If you were to meander through a cottage garden several hundred years ago, you'd be surrounded by plants that tower over their modern counterparts. They would also often have smaller flowers and shorter blooming time, so it is easy to see why plant breeders got to work, to increase showiness and make their dimensions more manageable. There was a tendency to breed dwarfer plants with larger blossoms. At the same time, merchants have always striven towards increasing the number of blossoms per stalk. And modern varieties tend to be self-branching whereas their older counterparts tended to shoot obstinately straight up or droop down.

Colours are more intense than they were a few hundred years ago. Compared to modern styles, an old-fashioned garden might have appeared relatively drab, with flower shades more subdued than at present. Another trait that has proliferated over the centuries is doubleness. We are often told that most old-fashioned flowers are single, but in fact that is not strictly true. Hollyhocks, for example, are one of the earliest documented frequent doubles, recorded in a wide variety of colours in the 17th century. The problem with double flowers is that they tend to be sterile – the reproductive organs fail to develop and look petal-like instead so double flowers can often only be reproduced by vegetative means. There are exceptions. If only the

The best way to be sure of the identification of a particular flower is to show it to others. Old catalogues can provide a fascinating starting point, but questions of identification must ultimately be referred to experts.

Noreen Jardine of Leamington Spa in Warwickshire, had long admired a sweetly scented rose in her elderly neighbour's garden, but she had no idea of its name. One day she was visiting a local rose garden and noticed that the China rose 'Cécile Brunner' looked very similar. However the young flowers of 'Cécile Brunner' seemed rather pinker than the delicate apricot pink buds of the rose next door, although the cabbagey open blossoms looked similar. Moreover the rose on display seemed to have a taller growth habit than the bushy rose she sought to name.

So Noreen consulted a well-known professional rose-grower who identified the rose as a coral sport of 'Cécile Brunner', known as 'Madame Jules Thibaud'. When Noreen contacted the National Council for the Conservation of Plants and Gardens (see page 84), they were delighted with her discovery and agreed to propagate the rose, ensuring its continuation – and donating proceeds from its sale to the continued work of the NCCPG.

Incidents like this show how gardeners can make sure that flowers do not disappear, regardless of changing fashions in garden design or trends in horticulture. Worthwhile sports do sometimes occur in nature, and with care they can be preserved for many generations to enjoy.

stamens are transformed into petals then they can be fertilised, although insects are rarely attracted, making hand-pollination necessary. Some flowers, such as primroses, stocks, paeonies and poppies, genetically tend to slip into doubleness. In the case of paeonies, doubling has been happening for a good two thousand years. But the first zinnias and marigolds were definitely single and some people treasure the simple single flower as the pure state. Each gardener has hos or her own fancies. But if doubles are continually preferred to the exclusion of singles they are in danger of disappearing.

The trait many gardeners miss most is fragrance. The fragrance in flowers has diminished considerably over the years. Florists are the culprits most frequently accused of taking the perfume from blossoms. Whenever flowers have been bred for the long stems that florists crave, they seem to lose their scent. There is little more disappointing than a florist's red rose, beautful in form and completely lacking in scent. It happened with sweet peas and sweet Williams. Even nosegay flowers such as violets became relatively unaromatic when florists began selecting for bigger blossoms and longer stems.

Breeders have been striving toward goals other than fragrance. When they work with flowering tobacco, for example, they go for a dwarf plant producing many showy flowers with interesting colours rather than the traditional pale tall deeply scented old varieties. When they work with freesias, they want to add blues and pinks to the colour spectrum. But most highly perfumed flowers are white, cream, yellow or pale pink; blue and red flowers aren't as aromatic. When breeders strive for maximum visual impact, fragrance is often forfeited.

FASHION COMES INTO PLAY

Any industry waltzes to the tune of supply and demand. If the public turns up its nose and refuses to buy 10 different campanulas, then seedsmen and nurseries quite naturally whittle down their inventory to the one campanula that has proved the most popular. Or if their audience crave clematis and purchase every plant that they can lay their hands on, nurseries and garden centres clamour to find and develop further clematis varieties.

"Old-fashioned" varieties have only recently been marketed with their history as a selling point. The term has more often had rather negative connotations. Plant buyers demanded the latest sweet peas and begged for new giant everblooming carnations – and could you blame them? If wilt-resistant double asters were to be had, then the public beat a path to the door of any supplier capable of fulfilling the promise. Who wouldn't seek out rust-resistant hollyhocks? Who wouldn't be curious to try improved double nasturtiums or dahlia-flowered zinnias? Newer varieties have often been developed to possess sought-after qualities. When, for example, cosmos was coaxed to bloom earlier in the season rather than flowering only briefly before being smitten by frost in autumn, who can blame tradesmen for rushing to carry the better product? But as the newest and the latest was offered, old faithful species and varieties went into decline.

Plant suppliers produce what they perceive their customers want, so we are all partly to blame when flowers such as the intensely fragrant Cupani strain of sweet peas become hard to find, upstaged by varieties that boast more blossoms and larger flowers on longer spires. We can all encourage healthy diversity by supporting specialist nurseries and demanding old-fashioned varieties from big commercial companies.

This old Austrian copper rose would grace any garden

Daylilies *Hemerocallis* and old-fashioned delphiniums form an attractive combination

National Council for the Conservation of Plants and Gardens

The mission of the British National Council for the Conservation of Plants and Gardens (NCCPG) is to "conserve, document, promote and make available Britain's great biodiversity of garden plants for the benefit of horticulture, education and science." Its best known achievement is the establishment of hundreds of National Plant Collections.

Enthusiastic amateur and professional gardeners hold these Collections, each of which aims to include the widest possible selection of plants within the selected genus, (species, subspecies, varieties and naturally occurring forms, along with their cultivars), and to ensure that they are protected from disappearing. The collections are all open to the public, some almost all the time, others with more restricted opening times.

Some people follow the philosophy that specialisation leads to extinction. The National Plant Collections show that the opposite can also be true – if there are lots of different specialists, specialisation can make sure that plants do not become extinct. The Collections currently conserve some 36,000 cultivars and 12,000 species.

National Plant Collection holders zealously guard our floral heritage, but an equally important part of their work is to make it available to others. Even if a gardener has the worthy ideal of choosing plants deliberately to ensure they don't slip away, it is hard successfully to pick a flower that you have never seen. Even if you have read lyrical descriptions and seen beautiful photographs, plants become so much more real when you can see them, smell them, discover ideal growing conditions at first hand. National Collections offer the opportunity for enthusiasts to do just this, providing not only the opportunity to see plants growing that might not be available anywhere else in the country, but also the benefit of specialist advice.

Although the NCCPG is principally organised along local lines, rather than through a centralised national membership, there are groups throughout the country. If you find that the National Collection of the particular plant that you favour is in quite another part of the country, and inaccessible to you, Collection holders are usually very willing to share their experiences and knowledge by letter or phone.

Among the many benefits of NCCPG membership is the chance to find out about, and attend, their plant sales. These are the most likely places to pick up treasures such as rare auriculas, the elusive double white rocket, rare perennial sweet peas or unusual clematis. It is quite a challenge to leave one of their sales empty handed.

The organisation also exhibits at national flower shows such as the Hampton Court Palace Flower Show where visitors can discover exciting plants they suddenly can't do without. But not all the plants are historic, the NCCPG is interested in diversity, in preserving our genetic heritage so that it can be used in future breeding programmes and scientific research, it looks forward as well as back.

As well as its role in preserving and multiplying the plants in its collections, the NCCPG is also actively involved in seeking out plants which are vanishing from gardens. In its early days at the end of the 1970s the NCCPG decided to compile and circulate a list of plants thought to be lost to cultivation in Britain, or that were at the very least no longer commercially available. This list has become known as the Pink Sheet since it was first accidentally copied onto pink paper.

The Pink Sheet lists endangered plants, and acts as an incentive for gardeners to locate the plants and propagate them for wider distribution. The current list includes many species from well-known and much-loved genera – five species of honeysuckle are listed, six species of daylilies, nine fritillaries including two white forms and nine species of perennnial sweet pea are among the entries. Sadly the annual *Tropaeolum minus*, the only nasturtium species grown in Britain for a century or so after its introduction at the end of the 16th century, is currently on the Pink Sheet. However, there is good news too, as the list also rejoices in the plants that have been brought back from the brink. Without the persistence and enthusiasm of the NCCPG, our floral heritage would be so much the poorer.

For details of the National Plant Collections and NCCPG membership please see Resources page 177.

FROM PAST TO FUTURE

When something becomes too popular it can spell its own demise. In a way this is what has happened to particular flowers, especially through the 1800s. During this century flowers became widely disseminated, the number of plants from abroad which could easily withstand the Northern European climate grew enormously, and cultivation of spectacular flower gardens moved away from the sole province of the rich. Gardening was enthusiastically taken up by all sectors of society. True, the poorer classes were less likely slavishly to follow a new garden design or fashion, but when a style or plant appealed it really took off.

Plants were being selected and improved continuously, but one result of this activity was the tendency to ignore old favourites in favour of ever more showy newcomers. Planting styles and bedding schemes evolved into something rather predictable, using vast numbers of a limited range of plants. Gardeners learnt how to extend the season of colour in their beds through using certain prescribed plants, and the formulae stuck.

By the middle of the 19th century even the grandest gardens seemed to be taken over by giant swathes of colour produced by relatively few species, and most small gardens were devoted to displaying a riot of annual colour through bedding plants. Consequently, towards the end of the 19th century it was already becoming difficult to find some old favourites, and even the most desirable hybrids of many of the florists flowers, for example, were only available for a short time as fashions moved on. Sometimes old-fashioned varieties may seem to have few attractions. Few gardeners, for example, would opt for the native achilleas when confronted with the numerous new forms and shades, while old-fashioned pinks and sweet Williams are a thousand times sweeter than modern ones. The first phlox were poorly shaped and in a limited colour range, there are now dozens of wonderful cultivars that most gardeners would prefer to adorn their borders. Conserving plants is not about keeping things purely for the sake of it, but once they're lost they're gone forever.

Gardens evolve, and presumably if certain good modern cultivars had been created earlier, gardeners would have used them. If the robust new 'Stainless Steel' aconite, for example, with its silvery spires of flowers and dark glossy foliage had been available in the 15th century, perhaps the native English monkshood *A. anglicum* would have been lost forever, yet it has its own charm, and its own place in history as well as in a modern garden.

Fortunately for plants, current garden fashions encourage naturalistic planting, balancing nature and the gardener's guiding hand. Whereas gardening trends first came from the Spanish world, then from Italy, and then France was very influential, England arguably led the way in gardening design for centuries. But new developments are coming from northwest Europe and North America where meadowlands provide inspiration, and there are opportunities to use other perennials and annuals to fill gaps between swathes of grasses and herbaceous plants.

Cottage gardens are also continually popular. In fact the climate is so right for old-fashioned varieties that several major catalogues have been inspired to mention the past of the plants that they offer. In some cases, a line is added to catalog text pointing out that a certain perennial has been grown for several centuries. Some nurseries and seed suppliers, especially companies that have remained in business for a century or more, have published specific lists of the heritage varieties that they still carry. Old-fashioned is no longer a negative term.

5

Spreading the word – propagation

Other children had chests of drawers full of sweaters and blouses, but mine were stuffed with marigold seeds. It all started with a packet of seed of mixed crested marigolds from the supermarket and a Brownie project. My goal was nothing more ambitious than to fill the backyard with marigolds, much to my parents' chagrin.

Being a child, and otherwise preoccupied, I neglected to deadhead as often as I should have done. This led me to discover that, if left to their own devices, the dried flowerheads contained a sheaf of seeds, and these looked suspiciously similar to the seeds in the supermarket seed packet. Dust to dust and seed to seed. This appealed to my frugal nature.

The marigold project continued year after year, leaving my drawers with less and less room for sweaters and blouses. And gradually the backyard scene also began to alter. After a while I didn't care so much for the bright orangeish-yellow marigolds. Instead, I favoured the deep brick-coloured version –

preferably with a tiny band of yellow hemming the edge of each petal and a crest in the centre. So began a very unscientific selection process.

I've moved beyond marigolds. Nowadays, sweet peas vie for space in the drawers. But there's a safeguard with sweet peas – they only remain viable for one year. On the one hand, I have the responsibility of harvesting enough seed for myself and friends annually. But after that season, I can toss out the leftovers in the cupboard with a clean conscience.

The only way to be certain of keeping any heirloom flower in the fold is to share it with fellow gardeners. That's how the original cottage gardeners kept their strains alive for so many years, and the same is equally true today. Throughout the centuries, gardeners have sent friends and fellow gardeners home with a handful of seeds or a cutting from their garden. Not only does their generosity ensure their popularity with the neighbours, it also helps to ensure that treasured flowers will be stewarded in other gardens and won't slip away.

ABOVE: Shining white old-fashioned 'Crystal white' single zinnias are much sought by seed savers

LEFT: Many favourite heirloom flowers are as popular with bees and other insect pollinators as they are with gardeners

Johanna Westgate's Wildflowers

Never let anyone tell you it's easy being a small nursery and seed supplier. Johanna Westgate says that there are days she'd like to give up her trowel and compost for good, times when she can't face saving another seed or dealing with another of the inevitable pieces of paperwork that any business generates. But most of the time she is happy doing what she loves, propagating plants and providing native flowers or their seeds to customers near and far.

Johanna had never intended to start a nursery. She grew up in lush English countryside, surrounded by wildflowers, but then she moved abroad and stayed away for 20 years. Upon her return she was saddened to see what was happening to the countryside, and in particular to the plants she loved. "I had never really thought about it," she said, "I just assumed everything would be the same as when I left." So she determined to do something about it.

Her small nursery is situated on the southern coast of England, in an isolated area near Romney Marsh, which boasts a large nature reserve preserving several hundred species of local plants. Much of Johanna's original seed was collected locally from plants growing wild on the Marsh; others were collected along the shoreline – Johanna is one of the few people raising sea peas and other maritime plants, preserving them from changing fortunes. Ten years on, and Johanna still collects some seed from the wild, the rest she raises herself. Her local town, Dungeness, was recently made famous by the artist Derek Jarman

who lived there and wrote about his seashore garden, encouraging further interest in Johanna's plants.

Over 100 different varieties of native and naturalised perennials thrive in pots in Johanna's tightly-packed nursery where not one inch of space is wasted. Her range extends to plants suitable for woodland gardens and for meadows, for wet habitats, and a specific range for what she terms "shingle gardens", or those close to the sea. Although she will supply seed to interested gardeners who can't get to her, the bulk of her business is in producing plants for sale at her premises and via a local co-operative that sells into larger outlets – her plants can be found at garden centres throughout Kent and Sussex. She doesn't provide a mail order service because there just aren't enough hours in the day.

Johanna is a campaigner. She wants to spread native plants as widely as possible; she also wants to encourage wildlife-friendly planting. You'll not find any chemical warfare in her nursery;she's never intentionally killed a slug or snail which she sees as "slow-moving lumps of protein" for blackbirds, frogs, toads, hedgehogs, slow worms and beetles. In a year when almost every gardener in Britain was lamenting a great slug outbreak Johanna had no problems: "My customers tell me it's been a terrible year for slugs. But I planted a salad garden for myself for the first time this year, and there was not a slug to be seen among the lettuces." She said that this might be because the blackbirds and other slug-loving creatures had

eaten them, but she thought it was due to companion planting with poached egg plant *Limnanthes douglasii*: "When I pulled up the poached eggs there were slugs snuggled into every plant. They might have liked the warm wet roots, they certainly never felt the need to move further." Johanna is always delighted to dispense such helpful advice "My gardening is not very scientific." But it certainly works.

When you purchase plants from Johanna they don't come with exhortations and very specific instructions; she has a surprisingly relaxed attitude toward most plants, refreshingly free of horticultural jargon. She says many plants are remarkably forgiving, and although wildflowers need to be managed in much the same way as many other old favourites, she doesn't want anyone to be frightened of trying.

Should you wish to know which plants to include in your garden to attract butterflies, Johanna will reel off an impressive list. Or what to plant by a pond. But she doesn't restrict her recommendations to wildflowers and has a very flexible attitude to cottage gardening, recommending that wildflowers be mixed with old-fashioned cottage garden flowers in abundant herbaceous beds. After all, our native wildflowers were the original floral gems of the garden.

If you visit Johanna's nursery you will come away enthused and ready to start a wildlife-friendly garden straight away. You will probably be carrying bat boxes and a bird table as well as numerous interesting plants. This is precisely what Johanna intends.

FIRST CHOICE – PROPAGATION

Plant propagation needn't be confined to professionals. Anyone can do it. For tools, you need nothing more complicated than a spade if you plan to divide your plant, a pair of secateurs for taking cuttings, or an envelope if you're collecting seed. And it isn't a particularly complex skill. Seed saving and plant propagating isn't a difficult science, but timing is everything.

When you find a plant that might possibly be an old-fashioned species or cultivar growing in a ruined garden or an abandoned estate, propagate it rather than digging the original plant. The same is true of wildflowers. Unless the plant is doomed to certain destruction through habitat alteration, leave the original plant unharmed. No matter how well you do it, transplantation can be traumatic to a plant. If it has survived for several generations in its current location, chances are that, however it appears, the location has proved a happy home for the plant. Overzealous collection has led to the extinction of a significant number of plants from our floral heritage.

BASIC PLANT PROPAGATION

Much has been written about different propagation methods - it's not a cut and dry science. You will find that many plants are extremely easy to propagate, although a few can prove more tricky. Every plant is an individual with its own needs and requirements. But that shouldn't stop you from attempting the feat.

If the basic method fails, try again at a different time of year or under different weather conditions. If a stem cutting doesn't work, try rooting a side shoot taken at its juncture. Give the cutting more or less sun, increase or decrease the humidity. Keep trying.

ANNUALS

The first factor to consider when sharing plants is whether you're dealing with an annual, biennial or perennial. Annuals survive only one growing season. In fact, in some cases – in severe desert climates, for example – ephemeral annuals sprout, grow, blossom, set seed and die in a few brief months. However, most of those annuals commonly available for garden purposes linger throughout most of the growing season. Among the best-known old-fashioned annuals are poppies, petunias, sunflowers, snapdragons and cosmos. Most annuals are propagated by seed. Sometimes their seed proves hardy (especially during mild winters) and seed scattered by the winds will germinate the following season. Love-in-a-mist, for example, usually self-sows, and old-fashioned flowering tobacco may do so but it isn't a reliable method of propagation. Annual flowers are usually the first to become-extinct when their popularity wanes.

That's where you come in. Gardeners keep annuals alive. In some cases, properly stored seed can last for several decades with only slightly diminished germination rates (the sacred lotus *Nelumbo nucifera* is reputed to remain viable for 1,000 years, although proof is understandably limited). Landscape historians often turn over the soil of a historic garden to encourage latent, deeply buried seed to germinate, helping them to find out what was grown in the garden centuries ago. Morning glory seeds remain viable for several decades but other annuals, such as sweet peas and other members of the legume family, go stale rapidly and the percentage of viable seed in a packet diminishes drastically after 18 months. Unless seed of those annuals is saved faithfully every year and replanted, the variety will slip away.

Old-fashioned sweet Williams *Dianthus barbatus* have much stronger fragrance than modern cultivars

PERENNIALS

Perennials grow from season to season. Some, including paeonies, dianthus, daylilies, roses and phlox, survive for hundreds of years as a testimony to past gardens and bygone trends. However, even perennials are not impervious to the traumas of time. Many lavenders and certain artemisias, for example, tend to be short-lived. Occasionally, a winter will prove so severe that a previously hale and hardy perennial suddenly perishes. It is wise to safeguard the future of perennials by sharing them with fellow gardeners. Horticulture is by no means a predictable science, so we need to hedge our bets.

Perennials are propagated by cuttings, divisions (if they form separate-rooted clumps such as mints, phlox and asters), or seed. However, there are a few caveats to saving seed of perennials. When you allow a plant to go to seed rather than deadheading it, this can weaken the plant and undermine its winter hardiness. Since the plant's purpose is to reproduce it throws all its strength into its progeny rather than fortifying itself to survive.

Also, if you allow a perennial to go to seed early in the season you are unlikely to get the benefits of a second, late-season blooming.

TENDER PERENNIALS

Tender perennials are usually treated as annuals because they are not winter hardy and frost kills them, though they will survive from year to year in a mild climate. They can be kept alive indoors throughout the year and some, such as pelargoniums, make excellent indoor companions over the winter. Many tender perennials can be propagated by seed, but if you want a heavily hybridised cultivar to come true you will have to take cuttings and protect them over the winter.

BIENNIALS

Biennials blossom during their second year and die back shortly after setting seed. However, their seed is often hardy and so a colony, once established, might continue in that spot year after year, although reappearance isn't as reliable as an established patch of a hardy perennial. Foxgloves, wallflowers and hollyhocks are biennial, although hollyhock plants may last longer than one season.

Biennials are propagated by seed, seedlings or divisions; they are rarely propagated by cuttings.

DIVIDING PLANTS

Division is one of the easiest ways of propagating plants, and is a useful way of reproducing hybrids that might not come true from seed. Divisions can only be accomplished if several separate crowns of a plant have their own roots. It is best to carry out divisions in the spring when the plants are small and upheaval will be minimal, and in cloudy weather when the plants will be least stressed. Take a trowel or spade, dig gently into the soil and pull apart a section of the plant keeping as many roots and as much soil intact as possible. Give the donor plant a generous drink of water immediately, and also sprinkle the roots of the division with water while you move it to its new location. Pot or replant the division immediately, watering it generously while the roots rejuvenate.

TAKING STEM CUTTINGS

Unfortunately, it is usually only professionals who take cuttings as many people think this is a difficult process, but it is easier than you may have been led to believe. Known as taking stem cuttings or slips, vegetative propagation is the method of choice for producing progeny of complex hybrids that might not come true from seed. Granted, there are a few plants that prove stubborn to propagate by cuttings, but many will take root without undue fuss or bother.

As a rule, take cuttings or slips when new growth has "hardened off", or when new shoots are firm and not so tender that they wilt easily. Early spring bloomers will produce new growth in summer after flowering, while cuttings from late season blossomers should be taken in spring.

The length of the slip depends on the type of plant you choose. Take a 3-4 inch (7.5-10cm) long sprig of a thickly foliated herb such as box *Buxus sempervirens,* but if a plant has several inches of bare stem between leaves, cut a longer stem with at least two leaves or sets of leaves.

Take cuttings on a cloudy day, watering the plant at least an hour or two beforehand. Bring the cuttings into a cool, shady place immediately. If you can't pot them straight off, wrap their stems in a damp napkin and slip them into a plastic bag, keeping them moist – most slips will survive for several days in these circumstances but the percentage that root will be diminished. Although some plants will root easily in a glass of water, these roots may adapt poorly to life in soil so it's wisest to root directly in sand, rooting medium or soil.

Remove the leaves from the bottom third of the stem. You can dip the bottom third of the cutting into rooting hormone, but in most case this isn't essential. Fill a small pot with a light, friable soil or sand (sand is best for difficult-to-root or hard-wooded cuttings such as rose sprigs) and insert the lower third of the cutting into the medium, firming the soil or sand around the base of the stem. All cuttings should be watered immediately and placed in shade.

To raise humidity and prevent wilting, place potted cuttings in a plastic bag, or under an overturned glass or bell jar. Keep the soil moist while the cutting is rooting. Depending upon the plant, roots should begin to form in 2-4 weeks. Repot the plant if necessary.

SAVING SEEDS

Cultivars and F1 hybrids won't come true to seed, but if it's possible to save seed from a plant, this is by far the most efficient and time-honoured method of propagation. It produces the most offspring and yields the most propagative material for sharing with gardeners near and far. Seed collection is rarely detrimental to the donor plant, but over-zealous collection can diminish a wild population, so be moderate.

POLLINATION

The first step in saving seeds is to make certain that the flower you're hoping to propagate becomes pollinated. A flower's stigma (female organ) must receive pollen from the anthers (male organ). If a species is self-pollinated, the pollen is transferred within the same flower and your chances of duplicating the plant precisely are excellent. But if a flower is fertilised by cross-pollination, like sunflowers, flowering tobacco *Nicotiana* and petunias, pollen must come via the wind, insects, or with your help from another flower.

The characteristics of most old-fashioned flowers have stabilised over years. Even if you are working with a cultivar, a large percentage of seed will come true if you make certain that your flowers don't cross-pollinate with a different cultivar nearby. But there are important exceptions: certainly families, particularly columbines and violets, cross-pollinate shamelessly. They will return in a range of different colours unless you take steps to keep a strain pure.

To increase the chance of true seed and prevent cross-pollination between two different species or cultivars, you can separate the plants by isolating them. Although there is little precise data about the distances necessary to prevent mingling, most seed savers feel that

Marigolds were popular plants in the 18th century, the old-fashioned scented leaf varieties are good companion plants

about 50 yards (46m) should do the trick. Physical obstacles such as solid fences or buildings also help in preventing contamination of seed. Or you can help prevent cross-pollination by staggering the times at which certain flowers bloom by sowing seed at separate intervals or in different conditions, or pinching one variety to encourage a later blooming date. These methods work best for flowers with a short blooming span. Seed set when two varieties are blooming simultaneously may be a mongrel between the two. Plants will seem like new plants but there will be variations in future generations.

To be absolutely sure that a flower does not cross-pollinate, cover the flowers with a paper or mesh bag and hand pollinate the flower yourself. If you have a sizeable plot and many flowers, you will need to cage the section with mesh screening to keep pollinators at bay. You'll have to pollinate the flowers personally, or you can let insects do the work by switching the caging on alternate days. Evening-scented and flowering plants such as tobacco plants and brugmansias are pollinated by night-flying creatures so keep their seed pure by covering from dusk until dawn and hand pollinating.

'Grandpa Ott's' Morning Glory

One of the best-known heirloom flowers in North America is 'Grandpa Ott's' morning glory, as it is one of the plants responsible for the establishment by Kent and Diane Whealy of the Seed Savers Exchange (SSE) in Decorah, Iowa, an organisation dedicated to preserving our plant genetic heritage. Initially concerned with vegetables and foodcrops, in 1989 SSE branched out into the Flower and Herb Exchange, specifically devoted to saving and exchanging seeds of the world's floral heritage.

Diane Whealy's Grandpa Ott didn't have to replant seed of his royal purple morning glory each year, the vine just self-sowed and sprouted up with no encouragement whatsoever. But that didn't stop Grandpa Ott from collecting seed. He was famed for his generous hand sharing the morning glory he brought with him when he immigrated from Bavaria to Iowa. "That was just his way," Diane remembers, "everyone who came to visit his little 40 acre farm went home with some of his morning glories." Grandpa Ott was the one who initially inspired Diane to save seed. He planted the first seeds, so to speak, of what has become Diane's great passion.

Once the Flower and Herb Exchange was established, Diane Whealy had to harvest her 'Grandpa Ott's' morning glory with some degree of certainty as other gardeners looked to her for seed. Cross-pollination was not a problem, 'Grandpa Ott's' was the only variety Diane grew, and anyway, morning glories don't readily interbreed. The main concern was harvesting seed before it shattered. "You have to keep an eye on the seed," she explains. "Morning glory seeds are held in little round buttons, they turn deep beige when they're ripe. And they shatter if you wait too long. I find myself picking every other day. When frost threatens, I lay a tarpaulin on the ground, pull up the vine and haul the whole mess into a shed."

Since she started the Flower and Herb Exchange, Diane has been harvesting seed of other flowers as well, each with its own set of concerns. The old-fashioned vining petunia, for example, forms a sticky seed pod that shatters at the slightest touch, releasing an uncollectible dusting of seed as fine as sand. "The nice part of growing seed is you don't have to deadhead your flowers all the time. But still, you have to be vigilant," Diane warns.

She never made a fine science of saving flower seed until recently. But she soon discovered she instinctively knew how to do the deed. She feels that most gardeners are the same. "Most gardeners are generous people," she's noticed, "they've often shared from their garden on a very informal basis." As any gardener knows, part of the joy of gardening lies in sharing your finds with friends near and far. This is how flowers are kept alive for generations.

COLLECTING SEED

Ideally, you should collect seed when it has fully ripened but its seed case hasn't yet shattered. Collecting seed too early isn't as irreparable as letting your seed scatter to the wind, as you can often ripen seed after it's been plucked.

As a rule, whatever their shape or style, seed pods darken as they reach maturity, and cases usually begin to look dry and turn papery. The trick is to harvest before they split – it's wisest to harvest with a napkin or something else that the seed can spill into, just in case the seed falls free of the pod while you're collecting. Some seeds, such as *Impatiens noli-tangere,* are notoriously prone to popping and even legumes such as sweet peas will shatter if you pluck them vigorously. If there's any danger of frost before fleshy seed pods or berries are ripe, harvest them green and bring them indoors for the duration of the ripening process, then remove the seeds.

SAVING SEED

Store your seed carefully. First make quite certain it is absolutely dry. High temperatures and direct sun can be damaging – never try a "quick dry" method in a microwave or oven, these can be lethal. Instead, spread the seed on a piece of paper or, ideally, on an elevated fine mesh screen in a cool, dry, airy (but not windy) place for a week or so, more if the weather was damp or rainy when you harvested. This is especially crucial for seed that has been removed from a moist fruit or berry (such as brugmansia or roses). Shuffle the seed around while it's drying to expose all sides to the air.

Keeping seed free of extraneous matter isn't crucial for amateurs who aren't selling by weight, but plant parts can harbour problems such as fungal spores of mildew and grey mould that might contaminate your seed and effect its viability. So try and sift your seed through a medium mesh screen before you store it. Then put your seed in a paper or glassine envelope, label it carefully, and store it in a cool, dry and dark place – an airtight canister is ideal.

SEED SOWING

Although most seed should be sown at the beginning of the next growing season, there are exceptions. Sweet cicely *Myrrhis odorata* seed, for example, must be planted immediately after it is harvested. Gentians, saxifrages and sedums should be sown in autumn. Many biennials are best sown the autumn after the seed is harvested and kept in a cold frame over the winter.

Sowing methods vary drastically depending upon the plant. Some like it warm, some like it cold; some (most larger seeds) should be covered, others (such as snapdragons and fine seed) are scattered on the soil's surface. Don't be disheartened if your seed does not sprout immediately. Some seed is frustratingly lethargic, particularly monkshood, bleeding heart, roses and Christmas roses. They can take a year to germinate. Try shocking them with a spell in the fridge. But don't give up.

HEIRLOOMS: THE NEXT GENERATION

When a flower has been in a family for several generations, an intimacy is achieved. Seed savers are privy to a plant's needs and eccentricities, and are usually very willing to share that knowledge. Most gardeners are proud of the heritage of their plants, and they are anxious to ensure their future.

Do your part to continue the chain unbroken. Keep plants alive for future generations by propagating them, by whatever method, and sharing them with other gardeners. Make certain that the flowers of yesterday are also the flowers of tomorrow. Pass them along.

Part Two

The Directory of Flowers

THE DIRECTORY — INTRODUCTION

Delving into the individual case histories of old flowers is fascinating.
Political intrigue, the life and death of kings, the conquest of lands and
the economy of nations have all been bound into the comings and goings of
blossoms. The unassuming little violet growing in your garden was once
grounds for arrest if you were seen wearing it. The meek anemone that
opens in spring once crowned the heads of Ancient Greek maidens. Plants
that are popular now were once avoided because of the superstitions that
surrounded them; flowers that were once commonplace have now vanished
without a trace. Nothing stays the same for ever.

Many flowers have been around for a very long time. As fashions came
and went, as gardening styles slipped in and out of vogue, different plants
became prominent and were prolific. Flowers we might scarcely consider
worth a second glance today once had their moment in the sun, champions
long before they were bred into the sleek, compact, multi-blossomed plants
of today with their impressive flower dimensions in vivid colours. But without those prototypes the modern developments would not be possible.

There are so many historically important plants that their members would
easily fill several thick volumes. We had to be selective when composing this
Directory. We chose only the key players, flowers most gardeners can enjoy
growing in their gardens today but it wasn't easy to winnow down the list.
For help with the task, we turned to one of the the earliest known seed and
flower catalogues, published in 1677 and issued by William Lucas of The
Naked Boy (see page 73). The plants included in that list formed the basis for
this Directory, but our list also includes plants popular long before The
Naked Boy began to trade, and long after it closed shop. Flowers evolve.

Some histories delve further back than others. Paeonies flourished in
Oriental gardens long before Europeans were aware that they existed.
Different civilisations have their own intricate floral history. An Egyptian or
Arabian perspective would be very different from a European view. But
when composing this Directory, it was necessary to select a vantage point
and since the British have been excellent chroniclers of horticultural history,
we have taken a European viewpoint. Most introductory dates mentioned
in the following entries stem from the first record of that plant in Britain.

For insights into the history of flowers, early herbals have traditionally
been consulted. Herbalists were the naturalists of long ago. Some of the earliest chroniclers of matters horticultural were the ancients such as Pliny the
Elder, born in Verona during the 1st century AD, and author of *Natural
History*, a 37-volume set. He perished watching Vesuvius erupt. And often
quoted is Theophrastus, a Greek philosopher born *c.*370BC and student of
Plato and Aristotle as well as the author of *Enquiry into Plants*. Charles de
L'Ecluse, or Carolus Clusius (1526-1609), was a Flemish humanist, doctor
and botanist who designed the Botanic Garden at Leiden where he was a

professor, but travelled broadly and wrote about what he found in *Rariorum Plantarum Historia,* published in 1601. Clusius was largely responsible for distributing many exotic plants through Europe, particularly bulbs, substantially changing the look of northern European gardens.

John Gerard (1545–1612) was born in Cheshire and looked after several gardens as well as creating his own in Holborn where he grew "all the rare simples" and "all manner of strange trees, herbes, rootes, plants, flowers and other such rare things." We have leant heavily on Gerard's *Herball or Historie of Plantes* published in 1597, which is why you'll find that date associated with many flowers in our Directory. The plant in question may have entered earlier, but we are certain that it was being grown by Gerard's day. Gerard's descriptions of the uses of many of these plants are known to be, at best, erratic, but they make a joy to read – his book is probably the most famous and popular English herbal.

Another milestone in horticultural history is John Parkinson's *Paradisi in Sole, Paradisus Terrestris* (Park-in-Sun's Park on Earth) published in 1629. Parkinson (1567–1650) was a British apothecary and gardener, and his work provides a wealth of plant descriptions and a reliable glimpse at the medical and culinary uses of yesterday's flowering plants. Nicholas Culpeper (1616–1654) was an astrologer and physician whose famous herbal has also been important; it provided a manual of herbal medicine for English housewives for centuries after its first publication in 1652. Philip Miller (1691-1771) was curator of the Chelsea Physic Garden from 1722 until his death, painstakingly chronicling all the plants he grew, and sharing his encyclopaedic knowledge in the *Gardeners Dictionary*, first published in 1731.

Records of early plant collecting expeditions have also provided much material - from the 17th century father and son team of the John Tradescants, through 19th and 20th century collectors such as Robert Fortune (1813-1880) and Ernest Henry Wilson (1876-1930). We have leant on 19th century catalogues and encyclopedias, and we are indebted to the scholarship of many modern day historians, chroniclers and – above all – gardeners. Fascinating insights have been gained through conversations and letters from holders of NCCPG National Plant Collections. They are keeping history alive, keeping our floral heritage safe for future generations.

The more you know about a flower, the more it comes to life and the more you can enjoy growing it. Use this Directory to increase that enjoyment. Look out for those old flowers, make them into favourites. Join the NCCPG, join plant societies, support specialist plant sales, look out for plants listed on the NCCPG Pink Sheet (*see page 84*). If your local nursery doesn't offer a specific plant, ask them to find it for you, or use *The Plant Finder* (*see page 188*) to discover a source. And when you're growing special plants, don't keep them to yourself but propagate them and pass them along. With your help, plants that are in danger of vanishing may be brought back from the brink. Above all, enjoy growing old-fashioned flowers, and use this Directory to help you on your way.

CONTENTS

Common names:

PERENNIALS & BIENNIALS

Acanthus mollis

ACANTHACEAE

bear's breeches

Acanthus came to Britain from Italy in the mid 16th century, but was well known to Southern European medieval herbalists as brank-ursine, used for a variety of purposes including soothing burns. The dark green shiny foliage is rather like exaggerated thistle leaves, and was widely used as a motif in classical architecture.

Acanthus are worth growing for their foliage alone, but the flowers are a great bonus: tall spikes of hooded pale pink flowers, rather like those of foxgloves, appear above the leaves in midsummer. Acanthus are easily grown in sun or shade in well-drained soil and can be propagated by seed sown in early summer or by division in late winter.

Recommended

A. spinosus: this was a slightly later introduction to England, in the 17th century. The leaves are more spiky and very deeply cut and it flowers more freely.

Achillea

COMPOSITAE

yarrow, pellitory, sneezewort, adder's tongue, pepperbox

Achillea takes its name from the warrior Achilles, who is said to have used the plants to staunch his warrior's wounds on the battlefield. The common British native *A. millefolium* was also used as a healing broth, said by Gerar d to be most often found in churchyards, reproaching people who ended up there because they had not drunk enough of it. *A. ptarmica* is a low growing British native with single white flower clusters in midsummer. Its peppery leaves were once used to ease toothache, and the ground roots taken as snuff. Its taller double form *A.ptarmica* 'The Pearl' is also known as shirtbuttons as it forms clusters of button-like flowers which last all summer long; similar doubles have been grown in British gardens for at least 400 years.

Achilleas are now available in such a multitude of colours and forms that few people give garden space to the good old forms, yet they definitely merit a second glance. Achillea are easy to grow in any well-drained soil, in sun or light shade, and easy to propagate by division in early spring.

Recommended

A. aegyptica (A. 'Taygetea'): Introduced in 1640 from the Middle East, pale cream flower heads blossom all summer on 2 foot (60 cm) plants with silvery grey foliage.

Aconitum napellus/Aconitum anglicum

RANUNCULACEAE

monkshood, wolfsbane, helmet flower

Native to Europe's damp woods and hedgerows, and listed as indispensable for 13th century physicians, monkshood was one of the most ornamental elements of monastery gardens, where it was used in a remedy for coughs. Most of the folklore that surrounds monkshood is based on its deadly qualities. One story says that the Aconite family is named from the ancient Greek word *akon*, meaning dart, because warriors impregnated their arrowheads with the lethal juices. Another tale is that monkshood sprouted from the saliva of the frothing jaws of Cerberus, the three headed guard dog of the Underworld, when he fought with Hercules on the hill of Aconitus. Arrows dipped in the juice of aconites were supposed to have killed wolves and badgers – hence the name wolfsbane.

Anglo-Saxons named the plant *thung*, meaning "very poisonous", and many early authors described the havoc monkshood could wreak – Gerard described a scenario in which an entire party perished when "ignorant persons" tossed monkshood leaves into the salad. However, Gerard's reports are notoriously unreliable and in fact there do not seem to be any records describing anyone ever coming to serious harm through monkshood poisoning, although the roots do contain strong alkaloids. Handling the plant gives some people contact dermatitis, and the poison can be absorbed through the skin.

Monkshood is a handsome hardy plant, with delphinium-like spires of large hooded deep blue blossoms and dark green palmate glossy leaves. *A. lycoctonum*, the yellow wolfsbane, *A. anglicum* (often listed simply as *A. napellus*) the violet native species, and *A. variegatum* (violet and white) were recorded in the 16th century. *A. album*, the graceful white flowered form, is another old variety.

Monkshood can be propagated by division in fall or early spring or from seed, planted as soon as it is mature. It thrives on neglect, and is best planted in moist soil in partial shade; it will grow in full sun but the foliage tends to yellow and the flowering period is short. Wash your hands after handling the plant.

Recommended

A. anglicum: a rare native still found wild in a few areas of south west England, with lilac blue flowers on 3 foot (1m) stems in May and June.
A. volubile: an unusual late flowering climbing aconite, introduced from Siberia at the end of the 18th century. Twining stems climb to around 8 feet (250cm) with clusters of dusky blue flowers in summer and autumn.
A. volubile needs shade and moist soil.

Alcea rosea

MALVACEAE

hollyhock

The hollyhock, with its towering spires of blossoms, is one flower that seems to embody the essence of the cottage garden. Native to China, holly-hocks were cultivated for centuries in the East before they reached England in the 16th century. It is possible that they first reached Britain centuries earlier with the Romans, but failed to thrive. *Hoc* is the Saxon word for mallow, and holy hoc may refer to their alleged arrival from Asia with the Crusades.

Once *Malva hortensis,* then *Althaea rosea,* hollyhocks are now called *Alcea rosea* from the Greek meaning "to ease or soothe". In the 16th and 17th centuries herbalists used hollyhocks like other forms of mallow, making a poultice from the leaves to ease pain and reduce swellings.

Contemporary gardeners often complain that double flowers have recent-ly taken over the market to the exclusion of older, single varieties, and they often cite hollyhocks as an example. Yet Sir Thomas Hanmer, writing in 1659, referred to growing single and double, white, pink, blush, scarlet, blood red, crimson and even black hollyhocks, so they are a notable excep-tion to the normal pattern of modern doubles driving out the old-fashioned singles.

By the early 19th century, the European market offered numerous named cultivars of hollyhocks (including a much-coveted striped sort) – one London nurseryman listed 80 named varieties in 1823. However, their fame was comparatively brief because they succumbed to hollyhock rust, and by the end of the 19th century there were few perennial hollyhocks and the cultivars that remained came to be treated as biennials or annuals.

Many of the most sought after old-fashioned hollyhocks are pastel shades of apricots and pinks; some of the most reliable and rust-resistant are forms of *A. ficifolia*, the fig-leaved or Antwerp hollyhock which came from the Eastern Mediterranean at the end of the 16th century. The closely related but less popular musk mallow, *Malva moschata*, is a hardier, more compact perennial European native. This has been grown in gardens since the 17th century.

Hollyhocks need plenty of room and thrive in well drained soil in mild areas. You can sow seed in early spring where plants are to flower, but bet-ter results are guaranteed by sowing seeds in containers in a cold frame in autumn and planting out in late spring. Always select seed from the best colour forms and take out inferior plants. Once established, hollyhocks will probably self-sow, especially in sunny spots in poor soil. If you have difficul-ty getting seeds established, try removing the small hollyhock plants carefully from the base of spent flower stalks at the end of summer and leaving them to overwinter in a cold frame for the winter. Set them out in their flowering positions the following spring.

Recommended

A. rosea nigra: has remained true since it was first cultivated around the beginning of the 18th century, producing gleaming purple-black waxy flowers in late summer.

Alchemilla vulgaris

ROSACEAE

Lady's mantle, lion's foot, nine hooks

Native to Europe, *Alchemilla vulgaris* was a valued wound herb for centuries before it was first named Lady's mantle in the 16th century by Jerome Bock, who associated it with the Virgin Mary. The Latin name *Alchemilla* comes from alchemy – it was once thought that the dew that collects in the centre of the fluted leaves could turn base metal into gold. It was also reputed to restore fading beauty. Stories relate that a leaf tucked under your pillow at night will guarantee sweet dreams.

Extremely hardy, *A. vulgaris* produces masses of tiny pale green flowers in early summer which last for months. Sprays are long-lasting in flower arrangements and equally suitable for drying. The similar *A. mollis*, often confused with *A. vulgaris*, came from Asia Minor in the 19th century; this is the commonest and some would say the best garden form. *A. erythropod*a, a dwarf form from the Carpathians, was introduced earlier this century.

Alchemillas are attractive and fresh-looking, grown largely for their fluted leaves which collect and hold onto drops of moisture from dew or rain. They are widely used to edge borders, grow well in sun or shade, and spread profusely.

Aquilegia vulgaris

RANUNCULACEAE

columbine, widow's weeds, granny's bonnets, doves round a dish

The European native *Aquilegia vulgaris* is a short-spurred blue columbine, cultivated in Britain since the 13th century. The names reflect the way the flowers resemble birds – *columba* refers to the stylised resemblance of the flower spurs to a flock of doves, *aquila* is Latin for eagle.

A. vulgaris and its various forms were the only available common columbines of cottage gardens until the 17th century. Gerard documents an upside down columbine with spurs at the tips of the flowers which survived into the 18th century but is no longer known to exist. In the 1600s, striped columbines were popular. William Lucas' catalogue of 1677 mentions the double form *A. vulgaris flore pleno*, and double or rose columbines have existed since the 16th century – 'Nora Barlow' is thought to have originated in the 1700s.

A. canadensis was brought to Europe from its home in the Canadian Rocky Mountains via John Tradescant the Younger in 1640. This long-spurred scarlet-flowering columbine was readily welcomed and revolutionised the look of European columbines. It was followed by *A. alpina* from Europe, from Siberia *A. sibirica* and then *A. viridiflora* from western China. The striking red *A. formosa* from Asia was another relatively early arrival.

Known to cross-pollinate readily, columbines must be segregated to remain true. Although plants are quite difficult to lift, division is the surest way to perpetuate a variety. Forms of *A. vulgaris* are the least likely to cross-pollinate, so you can collect seed from them with reasonable certainty. Seeds germinate best if sown immediately after collection, those kept until spring are less likely to succeed. Columbines prefer well-drained soil and dappled shade but they will also grow in full sun if the soil is well mulched to retain moisture, and will even prosper in deep shade.

Recommended

A. vulgaris 'Nora Barlow': a very appealing old-fashioned variety with very double or pompom style crimson, white or pink flowers, often edged with pale green. It thrives in sun or shade.

A. viridiflora: a scented variety from western China, with sage green and maroon-black long spurred flowers and strong golden stamens.

A. chrysantha: the popular golden columbine from New Mexico is a late flowering scented plant with attractive divided foliage and deep yellow blossoms. It was introduced into Europe at the end of the 19th century.

Aster

ASTER NOVAE-ANGLIAE / NOVI-BELGII

Michaelmas daisies

Cottage garden stalwarts, Michaelmas daisies are so called because they flower around Michaelmas, the end of September. In 1752, the Gregorian calendar was adopted and the feast of St Michael moved from early October to September 29th, and as asters were still flowering profusely then they became associated with the day and gradually became known as Michaelmas daisies. Most were introduced from America in the 17th century and became cottage garden favourites; those from New England took the name *Novae-Angliae* and those from settlements around New Amsterdam (now New York) were called *Novi-Belgii*.

The first Michaelmas daisy to be grown in England, *Aster amellus*, came from Italy in the 16th century. It came to be called blue starwort to distinguish it from common starwort *A. tripolium*, a British coastal native with yellow flowers. The flower most associated with the name Michaelmas daisy is probably *A. tradescantii*, an early 17th century introduction (via the John Tradescants) with large heads of tiny white daisy flowers on 4 foot (120cm) long stems. It is one of the last plants flowering in the herbaceous border, invaluable for flower arranging.

Michaelmas daisies were among the traditional cottage garden plants to be thrust into prominence by William Robinson at the end of the 19th century. The older varieties tend to flower longer and later, although modern forms may have more startling flower forms. They are all easy to cultivate, surviving most conditions – although mildew can be a problem so choose mildew-resistant cultivars. They prefer sunlight or dappled shade and reasonably moisture-retentive soil. Divide plants about every third year as the best displays come from young clumps.

Recommended

A. corymbosi: the heart-leaved aster was introduced from North America in 1765, with distinctive dark slender stems and neat foliage with sprays of small white daisy flowers.

A. dumosus: this dwarf form, particularly useful for small gardens, came from America in 1777. Very compact plants produce deep pink flowers.

Armeria

PLUMBAGINACEAE

thrift, ladies cushion, sea pink

Native to much of Europe as well as parts of Asia, North Africa and North America, *Armeria maritima* has certainly been grown in cottage gardens since the 16th century, most often used to edge paths. It was popular with Elizabethan gardeners for a while in their knot gardens, forming rounded tussocks of dark grassy foliage with bright pinky red flowers from May to July.

Thrift tolerates most soil types and weather conditions, including drought, but thrives most happily in well-drained soil in a sunny position.

Recommended

A. plantaginea grandiflora syn. *pseudarmeria grandiflora* has tufty dark green leaves with large bright carmine flowers on waving 1 foot (30cm) stems.

A. maritima alba: the white form of *A. maritima* has white ball flowers in early summer above clumps of dark green foliage.

Bellis perennis

COMPOSITAE

daisy, day's eye, bonewort, bruisewort

The name was originally Day's eye because the flower was the first to open in the morning, and close in the evening. It came into gardens at least 400 years ago, brought in from the wild. It was both added to salads and used medicinally as a poultice for bumps and bruises. Chaucer eulogised the daisy: "Of all the flowers in the meade, Then love I most those floures white and redde, Such that men call daisies in our town..."

By the late 16th century, there were numerous double-flowered forms in combinations of pinks, red and white, and this is when a popular sport, known as "Jackanapes on horseback" or the "hen-and-chickens daisy" appeared, its central flower surrounded by six tiny flowerlets sprouting from the base of the flower.

Daisies were popular Victorian cottage garden flowers, grown at the side of paths where their roots could enjoy the cool moist soil under the stones. Divide clumps when they are congested for better flower production.

Recommended

B. perennis 'Prolifera': the "hen-and-chickens" daisy has a centre flower from which six tiny flowerlets hang down – a mother hen surrounded by her chicks. All flowers are double, white with red tips.

Campanula

CAMPANULACEAE

harebell, bluebell, bellflower, Canterbury bell

Campanula means a tower of bells in Latin, and the family figures deeply in horticultural history. An age-old favourite is the graceful harebell, known in Scotland as the bluebell, *Campanula rotundifolia* (not to be confused with the English bluebell *Hyacinthoides non-scripta*), common for centuries in the Northern Hemisphere, and originally cultivated in France and Italy for its fleshy roots.

400 years ago every part of the campanula was pressed into service: leaves and flowers of several species of campanula were made into infusions and gargled to combat sore throats; lotions were made from all the vegetative parts to cleanse the skin; others were granted garden space ostensibly for purposes of feeding the family, even *C. persicifolia*, the peach-leaved bellflower, introduced into gardens about 1578.

The date when the creeping bellflower *C. rapunculoides* was introduced into Britain is not known, but some people associate the plant with the old legend of Rapunzel, who was imprisoned in a tower by a witch. One story states that her mother yearned for the plant during her pregnancy and sent her husband into the neighbouring witch's garden to appease her craving; when he was caught in the act, he was only released with the promise that he'd give his child up to the witch upon birth. *C. glomerata* is another European native grown by Elizabethan gardeners, *C. lactiflora* was introduced in 1814 from western Asia, and *C. latifolia* or giant bellflower was another Elizabethan favourite.

Native to Southern Europe, and introduced into British gardens in 1597, *C. medium* syn *C. media*, Canterbury bells, is a biennial that has always been popular in cottage gardens. Much to everyone's confusion, the now rare native *C. trachelium* was called Canterbury bells but for some reason, *C. medium* later took over that common name and *C. trachelium* became Coventry bells or nettle-leaved bellflower. The stems of *C. medium* are 3-4 feet (90–120cm) high, and thick, with sizable, inflated trumpets in shades of blue, rose, purple and red. The cup and saucer type, known as *C. calycanthema*, with a trumpet configuration similar to daffodils, is currently more often grown than the true species. There is also a double, flower-within-a-flower or hose-in-hose version in pink, white and blue. Hose-in-hose flowers usually date from Tudor times, reflecting the style of dress when men used to wear two pairs of stockings (hose), with the tops of the top pair rolled down over the other; hose-in-hose flowers looked as though one flower head was peeping out of another. Doubles featured in most 19th century catalogues in both blue and white, and are still available as *flore pleno* cultivars, although they are rare and difficult to establish. Plant the blue *C. medium* away from more strident blues, such as those of delphiniums, to appreciate its subtle colour and delicate shape.

The chimney bellflower or pyramidal bellflower *C. pyramidalis* was introduced from Italy and Austria before 1596. It has traditionally been grown in containers although it makes an attractive border plant as well in warmer gardens. It needs protection over winter in the ground, and it is best treated as a biennial, grown from seed or root segment cuttings. Although it can be a slightly demanding flower to grow, it is worth persevering as the tall pyramids of stunning blue flower spikes up to 6 feet (180cm) tall are impressive.

Campanulas are easy to cultivate and come in forms suitable for the edges and centres of borders, for sunshine or shade. Tall varieties may need support, particularly when they are young. Divide plants in spring to propagate or sow seed in autumn and overwinter under cover to plant out in spring.

Recommended

C. glomerata 'Crown of Snow': white clustered bellflower or Dane's blood is an atractive white form of the native wildflower, producing large clusters of white flowers in June and July.

C. persicifolia flore pleno: old double varieties of the Southern European native are rare but worth growing. Pale blue or white forms exist, some with very frilly double flowers, but they tend to be short-lived. They need to be planted in sunny spots in warm gardens.

C. trachelium: the nettle-leaved bellflower or Coventry bell produces clusters of licac blue bells around the stem. Grow it at the edge of woodland or in dappled shade. This is a delightful addition to any wild garden, flowering in June and July.

Cardamine pratensis

CRUCIFERAE

Lady's smock, cuckoo flower, bog spink

This common European plant is found in damp meadows, and along stream banks throughout the United Kingdom. Folklore associates the plant with fairies, so best left well alone – if a sprig was woven by mistake into a May garland, the whole garland would have to be undone and begun again from scratch. It is related to watercress, with similar leaves but with stems of flowers which are occasionally pure white but usually tinged with pale pink, or which may even be mauve or purple.

Lady's smock was grown for centuries to be used like watercress, as a salad herb or to flavour soup. Herbalists once recommended it as a cure for scurvy, and a lotion made from the plant was deemed to remove blemishes, and Dioscorides even recommended the juice of Lady's smock to relieve sunburn. The double form *C. pratensis flore pleno* was a very popular garden plant in the 17th century; like many doubles, this form is infertile so can't set seed but has to be increased by division in autumn. Lady's smock prefers damp conditions and partial shade.

Recommended

C. trifolia: introduced from Central Europe in 1629, small white flowers form in spring above dark leafed foliage which forms a dense mat in moist shady places.

C. raphanifolia: introduced into Victorian gardens, this rare naturalised Lady's smock has large deep lilac flowers in late spring.

Delphinium

RANUNCULACEAE

delphinium

Delphinium elatum was introduced in 1597 and is native from France to Siberia, but the delphinium hybrids we grow today are actually comparatively recent introductions, when they gained instant popularity. *D. elatum* was one of the primary players in the development of modern-day delphiniums: hybridisation began in the 1850s, with named varieties available by 1881. You can now find plants producing their distinctive tightly packed flower spikes in a wide range of colours – the stand of delphiniums at the annual Chelsea Flower Show is mouthwatering to any would-be cottage gardener.

Seed of some of the early-flowering cultivars has resulted in some especially good selections which have remained stable within a range of colours, although vegetative propagation ensures true reproduction of any cultivar. They thrive best in sheltered spots, or well-protected by other plants, in sunny spots in well-fed soil. Although some people are put off growing delphiniums because they need staking as they grow, this is a small price to pay for such a striking flower. If delphiniums are planted in a sunny sheltered position and the flower stalks cut back immediately after flowering, many cultivars will reflower, sometimes three times in one year with the first blossoms appearing in late spring and the latest in autumn.

Recommended

D. 'Alice Artindale': an old variety which is now rare. Smaller than many modern delphiniums, growing no more than $3^1/2$ feet (130cm), it produces very tightly packed spires of double lavender blue flowers.

D. delavayii: collected by the Catholic missionary and plant hunter Delavay in the 19th century. Growing to about 4 feet (120cm) tall, it produces narrow spikes of rich blue flowers in late summer.

Dianthus

CARYOPHYLLACEAE

pink, grass pink, clove pink, sops-in-wine, gillyflower, coronation/carnation, sweet William

Dianthus have been cultivated for millennia. They were much prized by the ancient Greeks, and the Athenians dubbed the plant Dianthos, Flower of Jove or Divine Flower (*dios* means god, and *anthos* flower). Over the centuries there has been much interbreeding, and the freely interchanged common names have not helped confusion over which earlier-named varieties correspond to later ones. Hundreds of years ago some dianthus were known as coronations or carnations because they were worn as crowns at festivals; carnations are commonly called pinks and *vice versa*. Gillyflower comes from the French, *gelofre* or *girofler* referring to the clove-like scent. They were believed to be called sops-in-wine because they were used to flavour wines and cordials, but this name has since come to refer to one particular old pink.

The development of pinks as cultivated flowers can be seen in many paintings from mediaeval times onwards, and they have been grown in British gardens since at least the middle of the 14th century. Queen Philippa, wife of Edward III, was recorded as growing "garofilus" among her herbs, no doubt referring to the early generic name *caryophyllus*. *D. gratianopolitanus* is the rare native British pink which has delicately scented small pink flowers covering soft grey foliage.

D. caryophyllus, the clove pink, is the parent of modern carnations. It originates in western and southern France but is no longer found in the wild. It is a single deep ruby red carnation with a marvellously heavy scent, and is much hardier than its progeny – most modern carnations are tender perennials, for all intents and purposes. *D. caryophyllus* was transformed from wild to highly cultivated flower very early on. Some authorities suggest that it was already developed within the Ottoman Empire before it was introduced to European gardens during the late 15th century. By 1629 Parkinson was writing of carnations that were striped, spotted and speckled, and in the 1700s an artist catalogued over 400 cultivars in three categories: 'Flakes' with two colours, 'Bizarres' with three, and 'Picotees' with a narrow band of colour around the edge of the petals. Unfortunately few of those striking carnations still exist.

Pinks were among the most popular so-called florists flowers (*see page 73*), developed by florists' societies throughout Britain in the 18th and 19th centuries. Much sought-after laced pinks, with delicate frilled edges, were developed in Paisley, Scotland, by the local weavers in the 18th century, and thrived for almost a century. By the middle of the 19th century there was such air pollution in the Paisley area due to increased industry that the pinks died out very quickly. Sadly, only a couple out of the hundreds of varieties raised by the florists of Paisley are still with us.

D. plumarius is the common or grass pink, a cottage garden favourite. The foliage is feathered, hence *plumarius*, and it sprouts in tufts, like grass. Gerard's twelve varieties of "wild gilloflowers" were all single-flowered and intensely aromatic common pinks. The oldest known hybrid is the highly scented cultivar known as 'Sops-in-Wine', introduced into England in the early 1300s. In the 1500s, "starre pinks" first appeared, frilly, single-petalled plants with dark pink eyes and overpowering scent, probably derived from *D. plumarius*. In the early 17th century, these "starres" spawned several notable hybrids with names such as 'Ragamuffin'.

D. barbatus, sweet William, is a biennial from the Pyrenees. The first written British reference notes Henry VIII's order of sweet William roots to plant at his newly acquired palace at Hampton Court. The name possibly honours William the Conqueror or perhaps commemorates William of Aquitaine. Single sweet Williams could be found in most cottage gardens from early days, as well as some double varieties such as the double scarlet 'King Willie' of 1634. All sweet Williams of the past were more scented than the varieties commonly available today, just one of the reasons for their loss in popularity; another reason is the fact they are quite difficult to place in the border as they flower very late in the season, in July and August.

The old vareties of dianthus are all very hardy as long as they are grown in a sunny position in well-drained soil, and they should last for many years if you cut them back in spring to encourage new growth, and encourage seedlings, or layer stems straight into the soil, with a little sand added, to produce new plants easily. Dianthus will rot if you let the crowns of the plants become waterlogged.

Recommended

D. plumarius cultivars: although some of these old cultivars are short lived, they are all worth growing for their scent and appearance.

'Nonsuch': a 16th century pink grown at Henry VIII's palace at Nonsuch, large shaggy single flowers are pink splashed with deep ruby.

'Mrs Sinkins': large double white to cream flowers have a wonderful perfume. These were raised in the 19th century by Mr Sinkins who was master of Slough workhouse.

'Sam Barlow': one of the commonest Victorian cottage garden plants, heavily scented double white flowers with a dark eye.

'Admiral Lord Anson': this 18th century rare carnation has double white purple fringed blossoms and a strong clove scent.

'Charles Musgrave', 'Musgrave's Pink' or 'Old Green Eye': believed to be an early 18th century survivor, pure white single frilled blooms surround a delicate green centre.

'Pheasant's Eye': this very fragrant late-flowering pink was grown in the 17th century; flowers are double white and deeply fringed with a deep purple eye and traces of lacing.

D. barbatus 'Nigracans': this deep maroon-flowered, dark-leaved variety from the early 19th century is much more scented than modern sweet Williams.

Dicentra spectabilis

FUMARIACEAE

bleeding hearts, Dutchman's breeches

Not an ancient plant by any means, the bleeding heart didn't appear in cottage gardens until the mid 19th century, but it immediately became popular. The foliage is lacy and handsome and the flowers are plentiful and whimsical: two pairs of flower petals form the bleeding heart – the outer pair form the heart and the inner pair resemble the drop of blood as the heart opens to reveal the stamens inside. Native to Siberia and Japan, the hardy *D. spectabilis* was first introduced into Europe in 1810, but apparently failed to thrive until it was reintroduced as recently as 1846 by Robert Fortune who found it cultivated in a Chinese garden.

Plant bleeding heart in moist well-drained and well-mulched soil in partial shade for best results. Clumps can spread for 20-30 feet (6-9m), with flower stems over 4 feet (120cm) tall, although it rarely attains these dimensions. Bleeding heart makes a showy specimen plant in late spring and early summer, and looks particularly well if underplanted with mat forming perennials or where tall perennials will grow up and cover its dying foliage from midsummer onward. The lower growing *D. formosa*, introduced in the 19th century, can be very striking planted in front of *D. spectabilis*.

Digitalis

SCROPHULARIACEAE

foxglove, fairy's gloves, fairy thimbles, virgin's glove

Digitalis purpurea, the common foxglove, is one of Britain's best known native plants, and different species of digitalis are found throughout Europe, North Africa and even Central Asia. Handsome perennials or biennials with spires of tubular blossoms (which could be said to resemble a cluster of gloves), they were originally called folksgloves throughout much of Europe, an allusion to the fairies that shared their woodland habitat. For centuries *D. purpurea* has been as commonly grown in cottage gardens as on the great estates.

Digitalis was always widely used in country medicine, but not originally for heart-related ailments. Instead, it was prescribed for healing "those who have fallen from high places" by Gerard and for sores and ulcers by Parkinson. The story goes that a witch (probably a local folk healer) passed the secret of digitalis to the doctor William Withering in the 18th century.

His experiments led to the discovery of its use as a heart stimulant, for which some species of digitalis are still commercially cultivated today.

Foxgloves prosper in shade on the edge of woodland in the wild, so plant them in dappled shade in the garden, although *D. purpurea* will tolerate more shade than other species. Traditional cottage gardeners particularly valued the white varieties of foxglove such as *D. purpurea albiflora*, and those sporting noticeable throat markings. Nowadays, the trend is toward stockier plants that bloom the first year, such as 'Foxy', as well as strains with blossoms surrounding the stem rather than being one sided.

Foxgloves always seem to flourish unaided in other people's gardens. But despite the fact they self-seed profusely, foxgloves are not always easy to establish in a garden and it can take many years to get a colony growing happily. Seed can lie dormant for years so the most reliable way of ensuring success is to collect some seed as soon as the capsule splits in late summer and sow it straight away in pots, overwintering in a cold frame for planting out in early spring. Seed requires light to germinate, so simply press it into moist compost. To ensure that seed comes true you will need to grow particular foxglove species in isolation and rogue out colour variants as they occur – *D. purpurea* forms, for example, will often include a percentage of reversions to the dominant purple colour; if you are a ruthless colour controller these can be removed as soon as they begin to colour.

Recommended

D. grandiflora: the great yellow foxglove is a compact and very easy perennial hailing from Eastern Europe, believed to have first arrived in Britain in 1595, although more reliably recorded from Turkey in 1738. Soft yellow flowers form densely packed 2 foot (60cm) spires, excellent for naturalising in sun or shade.

D. lanata: arriving from the Balkan peninsula in the 18th century, this architectural perennial foxglove has pale brown flowers with pronounced white lips, and hairy stems. *D. lanata* is the chief source of the heart drugs *digoxin* and *digitoxin*.

D. lutea: a native of central Europe and Italy, *D. lutea* arrived in Britain in 1753; its wiry but elegant 3 foot (1m) stems are packed with small pale yellow flowers.

Echinops

COMPOSITAE

globe thistle

Echinops is Greek for hedgehog, which sums up the appearance of this prickly plant which is crowned by white or blue spiny globes. *E. ritro*, native to Southern Europe and introduced into Britain by 1570, has felted, thistle-like leaves topped by blue-tinted globular flowerheads. By the 19th century it was upstaged by *E. ruthenicus* from Russia, with shiny green leaves with silvery downy undersides and larger, deeper blue flowerheads.

Echinops was a common Victorian plant, particularly in larger gardens, and is a stunning architectural addition to any border, but give it space to grow. Plants are not very fussy about soil as long as they are planted in a sunny position. They can be propagated by seed or by division.

Erysimum cheiri

CRUCIFERAE
wallflower, wall gilliflower

Erysimum cheiri (formerly *Cheiranthus cheiri*), the wallflower, is a southern European native, known to have grown in ancient times throughout all Mediterranean lands. Their name is believed to derive from the Greek *cheir*, meaning hand, alluding to the bouquet of wallflowers that was traditionally carried by young women and girls at many ancient ceremonies. Despite their origin, they didn't come over to Britain with early conquerors but were only introduced in the 1600s. Although originally perennial in Southern Europe, wallflowers grow as biennials in Britain.

Wallflowers have always been willing colonisers, thriving, as their name describes, on old walls and on stony ground. As with all gillyflowers, the early varieties were famed for their wonderful aromatic scent, a special treat in early spring, as wallflowers bloom from the cold days at the end of winter right through to the heat of summer. Some of the older varieties bloom from late autumn right through a mild winter.

The earliest wallflowers all bore single yellowish orange flowers, rather similar to their humbler wild mustard relatives, but with a sweet and powerful fragrance. Double varieties were appearing by the 17th century, and by the 19th century – the heyday of the wallflower – cottage gardens boasted cultivars in shades of red-brown, yellow, crimson, orange and cream.

Wallflowers fell out of favour with gardeners this century, probably because more and more varieties were produced in astonishing colours and forms, but completely lacking the scent which was once the prime reason for growing these early spring blossomers. However, some older varieties are available, proffering fragrant flowers on robust hardy plants which flower over a long season.

They thrive in poor or moderately fertile well-drained soil in full sun, and are perfectly happy on old paths and ruined walls once established. Sow seed in a cold frame in spring and transplant to flowering positions in autumn. Trim plants lightly after flowering so they don't get too leggy.

Recommended

Erysimum (Cheiranthus cheiri) 'Harpur Crewe': dating from Elizabethan times this was rediscovered last century by the Reverend Harpur Crewe. Intensely fragrant double and semi-double yellow flowers grow on plants 12–18 inches (30–35cm) tall, flowering from April to July.

E. 'Bowles Mauve': A vigorous evergreen perennial with narrow grey-green leaves and fragrant mauve flowers from late winter to summer.

Geranium

GERANIACEAE

cranesbill

The seedhead of many hardy geraniums is shaped liked a crane's bill, hence
the name, from the Greek *geranus*, crane. Some hardy species such as the
woodland native *G. sylvaticum* (king's hood or mountain flower) and meadow cranesbill *G. pratense* have grown wild in Britain for centuries, brought
into gardens before the 15th century. The annual *G. robertianum*, herb
Robert, is mentioned in mediaeval chronicles; *G. macrorrhizum* and *G.
tuberosum* were in cultivation by the 16th century, *G. versicolor* and *G. argen-
teum* in the 17th century and others followed – about 300 species of cranesbills are found, in all except very wet habitats, throughout temperate
regions. Some half hardy species come from warmer areas. Undoubtedly
there are cranesbills to suit almost every gardening situation.

Different geraniums have been in vogue through the centuries, from the
few species known in Elizabethan times to the hundreds by the Victorian
age, and an ever-increasing number today. There are huge variations in the
plants, some low-growing and shade-loving, others taller or mound-forming
and happiest in sun. Traditionally, many of their number have been used as
excellent ground cover plants; they flower freely producing attractive bowl
shaped flowers and their distinctive foliage often has good autumn colour.
They tolerate most soils, unless waterlogged, and are easily propagated by
division in spring.

Recommended

G. pratense album: this white-flowered form of the native meadow cranesbill
is a good herbaceous plant forming large clumps up to 3 feet (1m) tall and
flowering freely from June right through until September.

G. macrorrhizum album: grown in gardens since the late 1500s and good for
dry and shady places. It has very pale pink flowers and forms thick 1 foot
(30cm) tall mounds of scented foliage which turns brilliant red in autumn.

G. sylvaticum 'Mayflower': this attractive form of the native woodland geranium produces clusters of pale lavender-blue flowers tinged with pink,
above wavy 2 feet (60cm) stems.

Helleborus niger

RANUNCULACEAE

Christmas rose

Despite its attractive name, the Christmas rose was much used as a poison by
the Greeks. All hellebores are poisonous, but this didn't stop 16th century
herbalists from using the British native *Helleborus foetidus* (stinking hellebore)
as a common vermifuge, though it may as often have killed the patient as
the worms. Native to Central Europe, some say the Christmas rose came to

Northern Europe and Britain with the Romans, but it is first recorded in England in the 16th century. It produces saucer-shaped white flowers, sometimes tinged with green or pink, in mid to late winter.

Hellebores like light shade, they tolerate most soils but are greedy feeders so enrich your soil with plenty of well-rotted farmyard manure before planting, and mulch plants well so they don't dry out in summer. To increase stock, divide clumps after flowering, in late spring.

Hemerocallis

LILIACEAE

daylily, asphodel lily, lemon lily

Today daylilies come in a wide range of colours, shapes and sizes, but the proliferation of hybrids is actually a 20th century phenomenon, begun at the turn of the century by the British gardener George Yeld and mushrooming in the 1940s. Two millennia ago Greeks were familiar with the rust-coloured *Hemerocallis fulva*, which probably originated in China and Japan where the flowers were harvested for the table, added to meat dishes and soups. Another ancient daylily is the intensely fragrant yellow lemon lily, *H. lilio-asphodelus* (formerly *H. flava*), grown in ancient Egypt and Rome, and mentioned by Dioscorides as a medicinal herb in the 1st century.

Arriving in Britain in the 1570s with the immigration of French Huguenots, hemerocallis were grown extensively in gardens. They made themselves quite at home, were fruitful and multiplied - the foliage was used for fodder, recommended to increase milk production in cows. Double hemerocallis appeared in Britain as early as 1576, common in China long before then.

Hemerocallis were appreciated in Britain, but they truly found a happy home in North America. By 1695, they seemed to be everywhere, adopted by every wave of immigrants that arrived, common in every ethnic garden. And that might explain why hemerocallis, especially *H. fulva*, is now naturalised. In many parts of North America it has reached weed status, lining the streets and bedding bankings with orange blossoms that tend to clash with other flowers.

The introduction of *H. aurantiaca* from China in 1890 changed the destiny of hemerocallis. *H. aurantiaca* displays a tinge of red and, although it's self-sterile, it successfully expanded the colour spectrum for day lilies. Meanwhile, the blue daylilies that 19th century gardeners once adored were later reclassified as funkias, which then became hostas. Blue remains an elusive shade for hemerocallis.

Known for their robust nature, daylilies are easy to grow, but should be planted with the roots spread out and the crown of the plant no more than 1 in (2.5cm) below the soil as they don't flower so well if they are buried deep. They should be propagated by division in spring or autumn – you will know when to divide them when the plants produce less flowers than in previous years. They also set seed with little provocation, which has led to the onslaught of daylilies currently available. Modern hybrids are the easiest of all to grow, but the species also thrive in moisture retentive sites in Northern European gardens.

Hesperis matronalis

CRUCIFERAE

sweet rocket

This Southern European native arrived in Britain very early on to grow wild in marshy fields, from where it was brought into the garden in the 14th century to become a popular cottage garden plant. The Greek *hesperis* means evening, referring to its wonderful evening scent, and although its existence in early utilitarian gardens was justified by herbalists' use of sweet rocket to bring out a fever, it has always chiefly been grown as an attractive and fragrant addition to any border, with simple flowers in white, pale pink, or shades of mauve. Gerard and others particularly praised the double flowered white form, *H. matronalis flore pleno,* which can once again be found at specialist nurseries after a period of near extinction. It is a brilliant shining white flower, shown to its best advantage when planted against dark leaved plants.

Sweet rocket is perennial in rich loamy soil, otherwise it is short lived but self-seeds profusely. It is happy in sun or light shade. Single forms can be propagated from seed; double forms are more difficult to spread and require careful division, or you can try to remove the small offshoots from the base in spring and grow them on separately, although these are quite difficult to propagate successfully.

Recommended

H. matronalis flore pleno: attractive double forms are still rare, and the flowers are rarely pure white, more commonly a very pale pink bleaching to white as their flowering period progresses. The truly white double *H. matronalis flore pleno* 'Nivea' was listed as an endangered plant on the NCCPG Pink Sheet (*see page 84*), but is now available from a small number of nurseries.

Iris

IRIDACEAE

iris, bearded iris, sweet flag

One of the oldest known plants in cultivation, iris were already blooming on Minoan walls in 2000BC. The Ancient Greeks believed that Iris was the messenger of the gods and the personification of the rainbow; among her duties was the task of leading the souls of women to the Elysian Fields – for that reason the Greeks planted purple iris on the graves of women.

The iris has often appeared in heraldry as a symbol of power, and the fleur de lys was originally a conventionalised form of iris, not a lily as many people have suggested. Apparently in 1147, shortly before setting out on his ill fated crusade, Louis VII of France adopted the purple iris as his device in obedience to a dream, and so the fleur de lys came to the banner of France.

Different species of iris have had numerous medicinal uses throughout millennia. Dioscorides' *De Materia Medica*, the main influence behind herbal medicine for at least 1500 years, begins with an article on *I. germanica*, the bearded iris, followed by one on *I. pseudacorus*, the yellow flag or water iris. *I. pseudacorus* had many uses other than medicine (or ornament) for centuries in Britain – peasants made inks and dyes from the roots, they used them in an infusion for brewing, and used the swordlike leaves for caning chairs and even thatching roofs. *I. pseudacorus* makes a magnificent display of tall (to 5 feet/1.5m) yellow flags in May and June if grown in moist conditions.

Dioscorides suggested that orris root, the powdered root of *I. germanica* 'Florentina', should be drunk with honey, vinegar, or wine to ease coughs and colds, "torments of the belly", and much more, while poulticed orris root was good for ailments ranging from ulcers to broken bones and headaches. The violet-like perfume of orris root was widely used in perfumes from ancient times to mimic or bring out the scent of violets; it continued in use right up till the mid 20th century when an artificial substitute for the violet fragrance was created. Among its many uses as starch and perfume, one of its most bizarre uses was as the powder used to stiffen enormous fanciful hair arrangements in the 18th century, so they could stay in place for weeks or even longer.

Four hundred or more species of iris grow in the Northern Hemisphere. Of these the British native *I. foetidissima* is still worth growing for its vivid decorative open seed pods which split to reveal glowing red seeds – hence the names adder's mouth and dragon's tongue; its leaves smell of raw meat when crushed.

I. pallida, sweet flag, has grown in Britain since 1580, producing lilac blue fragrant flowers in early summer, and wild blue and white forms of the daintier water iris *I. sibirica* have been found in Britain since the late 1500s. While *I. germanica* has a long history, it was not a parent of the modern tall bearded iris which are progeny of *I. pallida* and *I. variegata*. All modern bearded iris have been developed in the last 150 years.

The iris family display a huge range of variations: most have rhizomes but some have bulbous roots; some are content in dry soils, others require damp or wet conditions; most require sun. Bearded iris are among the easiest to grow, thriving in well-drained soil with their rhizomes barely covered. To propagate them, dig up the rhizomes after flowering and select two small rhizomes growing at an angle from the large one that bore the flowering stalk. Discard the large part, cut the small rhizomes off with a sharp knife and plant them just under the soil leaving them partly exposed.

Recommended

I. pallida 'Dalmatica': a very attractive form dating back to the 17th century. The flowers are soft blue and scented, with yellow beards.

I. persica: from Turkey and central Asia, a bulbous rooted dwarf iris which flowers from late winter through to mid spring. Flowers are silvery grey to sandy yellow or pale green, with contrasting darker markings at the tips.

I. pumila: this dwarf bearded iris has grey green leaves and in mid spring the unbranched stems bear solitary scented blue, purple or yellow flowers.

I. sibirica 'Perrys Blue': this attractive beardless iris has striking dark blue flowers. Created in 1921, it is now hard to find.

Lupinus

FABACEAE

lupin

Native to the southern Balkans and the Aegean, the annual, 4 foot (1.2m) tall, white flowered *Lupinus albus* (white lupin or wolfbane), has been grown since ancient Egyptian times; it was originally grown as fodder, a purpose for which it's still planted in Italy and Sicily. The old cottage garden lupin, the North American or Virginian lupin *L. polyphyllus* was brought to Britain by John Tradescant in 1637. Most often it has spires of blueish purple blossoms, with infrequent white, pale pink and even bicoloured forms. Another early European lupin was the smaller *L. luteus*, valued for its intensely fragrant yellow blossoms.

The modern many coloured lupins so popular in gardens are very different from the old-fashioned plants; most are Russell lupins, named for their breeder George Russell, who was inspired by a display of lupins at the coronation of George V, and then worked on the plant for 25 years. In 1937, his strain was first put on public display; the plants included red, deep pink, orange and yellow monochromatic flowers as well as several dramatic bicolors which completely overshadowed the species formerly grown. Many of the early Russell lupins deteriorated over several decades but they have been reselected to form plants with even better colour.

Russell lupins have tall 1¹/2-2 foot (40–60cm) spires plump with pea-like blossoms in an astonishing range of colours, and that's undoubtedly why they've taken cottage gardens by storm. We continue to want them in our gardens despite the fact that their blossoming period is short, although they will usually reflower if you remove the flowerheads before the seed sets.

They are also very susceptible to slug damage in a damp spring and they tend to attract aphids in a hot summer. But even if they are damaged by pests, lupins usually rally the following season, although an individual plant rarely survives longer than half a dozen years.

Propagate Russell lupins by division, but lupin species should be multiplied from seed which should be nicked and soaked for best germination. Species cross-pollinate easily, so you may wish to isolate strains. Lupins are not fussy about soil and will grow in full sun or part shade. *L. polyphyllus* and its progeny are poisonous.

Lychnis coronaria

CARYOPHYLLACEAE

rose campion, gardener's delight, mullein pink

The rose campion *Lychnis coronaria* is the flagship of the lychnis family, believed to be the plant that inspired Theophrastus to affix the Greek name stemming from *lychnos*, or lamp – which some authors feel alludes to the vivid magenta blooms and others suspect is connected with the downy leaves, once used in making candle-wicks. The date of its introduction from Southern Europe to more northern areas has been lost, but we know it has grown in British gardens since the 1300s. The white form was also a common garden plant in Gerard's time and still exists, in the wild and cultivated under the name of 'Alba'. By 1614 there was a double magenta and by 1665 a double white form was available, but the doubles were reported as rare by the mid 19th century.

L. chalcedonica, or Maltese cross gained its common name from the legend that the plant, native to Russia, was brought by Louis IX to France from the Holy Land. It is very striking, resembling a cluster of scarlet Maltese crosses, so it was admitted into early gardens even without obvious medicinal uses. A double scarlet variety was introduced by 1629 and became widespread although it could only be propagated by division or stem cuttings and had a tendency to revert to the single state. It was already rare in 1835 and is now difficult to find. By 1710, there were white and flesh-colored forms. A double white is now rare.

Lychnis flourishes in well-drained fairly poor soil and can be propagated by seed or division. Rose campion seeds itself shamelessly but is easily pulled up if it grows where it is not wanted.

Monarda didyma

LAMIACEAE

bee balm, bergamot, Oswego tea

A native North American prairie flower, this species is named after the Spanish botanist Nicolas Monardes who, in 1571, wrote of the virtues of American medicinal plants. It first flowered in England in 1745 after the seed was sent from Oswego by John Bartram to Peter Collinson.

Although a few garden varieties are forms of *M. fistulosa*, the lavender flowered wild bergamot, most originate from *M. didyma*. In the wild this plant reaches up to 6 feet (1.8m) tall, with clusters of long tubular bright crimson flowers with red tinged bracts, sitting above square stems. Bergamot was traditionally made into a tea by the Oswego Indians who lived by the shores of Lake Ontario, and this use earned it a place in history as Oswego tea was drunk by American patriots during their struggles with the British over import duties on Chinese teas.

M. didyma will grow in a variety of soils and conditions but prefers lightly shaded moist areas of the garden. If grown in full sun, mulch with well rotted compost in April to conserve moisture. Divide clumps every third year or propagate using the rooted side shoots. Seeds can be grown in a cold frame in the autumn for planting out the following spring.

Recommended

M. didyma 'Cambridge Scarlet': one of the oldest cultivars, introduced at the end of the 19th century, with very rich red flowers.

Myositis

BORAGINACEAE

forget-me-not

Forget-me-nots are widely distributed throughout Europe and Asia, their small bright blue five petalled flowers appearing in cottage gardens for hundreds of years. Although there is an annual or biennial form, the fabled and most common forget-me-not is the perennial *M. scorpiodes* or *M. palustris*. Legend suggests that it received its common name because a knight drowned while fetching the flowers for his beloved, and as he slipped into the water he cried "Forget me not". But the name can just as well apply to the fact they spread rapidly and appear even in places from where you think you have removed them. The genus name *myositis* comes from the Greek *mys* for mouse and *otis* for ear, referring to the plant's small folded leaves. *Scorpioides* refers to the fact that early herbalists believed they were useful against the bites of a scorpion and other venomous bites.

Despite their ancient history, forget-me-nots were left to themselves for centuries and it wasn't until the 19th century that they came to the attention of breeders. Then an attractive white form was developed with a tidier habit than the blue, ideal as bright underplanting in shady or damp borders. Perennial forget-me-nots will flower from spring through the summer, but once they set seed the leaves tend to get mildew and plants should be pulled out. Forget-me-nots run happily among other plants to provide welcome mats of bright blue or white in places in the garden where other flowers may be harder to establish.

Grow blue forget-me-nots from seed sown indoors in early spring. They need darkness to germinate so cover the tray until seedlings appear. Once established in a border, they will self-seed freely however ruthlessly you thin them. The white form should be propagated through cuttings, although seeds may also come true.

Nepeta

LABIATEAE

catmint, catnip, catnep

Catmint or catnip *Nepeta cataria* is a hairy leaved British native, grown in gardens for many centuries, with slightly insignificant creamy white flowers on felty grey green leaves, but a strong scent much loved by cats. Grown in British gardens since 1265, cats are often strongly attracted to the plant but if you wish to dissuade them the ancient wisdom is to plant seeds rather than transplanting cuttings: "If you set it, cats will get it; If you sow it, cats won't know it."

Before tea was imported from China, catnip tea was a popular stimulant among the lower classes. Also, mice and rats are reputed to despise catnip, so it's occasionally grown as a companion plant to vegetable crops, although there seems little or no proof that it is effective.

The catmint that parented the nepetas we now grow as ornamentals is of fairly recent vintage. *N. mussinii* arrived in Britain from the Caucasus in 1804 or so, illustrated in the *Botanical Magazine* in 1806. *N. mussinii* then crossed with the less hardy *N. nepetella* (from North Africa) to give us a series of hybrids known as *Nepeta* x *faassenii*. They are impressively hardy and their abundant flowers range from mauve to pale purple, almost hiding the blue-grey to green leaves.

Catmints are extremely easy to grow, in any well-drained soil in a sunny position. They will grow in partial shade but won't flower so well. Propagate by seed, division or taking softwood cuttings in autumn.

Recommended

N. sibirica (syn *Dracocephalum sibiricum*): coming from Siberia and Mongolia in the 18th century, it produces striking upright spikes of rich blue flowers all summer long, with tidy clumps reaching up to 3 feet (90cm) tall.
N. govaniana (*Dracocephalum govanianum*): another unusual form, also tall and clump-forming, producing long panicles of creamy yellow flowers from midsummer to early autumn. It likes partial shade and more moisture than other catmints.

Oenothera

ONAGRACEAE

evening primrose

Parkinson described *Oenothera biennis* as the "tree primrose of Virginia" when recommending it to cottage gardeners in 1629. A tender perennial or biennial, in its second year 3-4 feet (90–120cm) tall flowering wands appear, topped by short-lived broad primrose yellow flowers. The scented flowers are tightly shut during the day, but open during late afternoon, and although they last a very short time, they flower repeatedly over several months.

Evening primroses were first cultivated in Europe for their tender young roots which were apparently eaten like salsify. But by the 19th century most Northern European gardeners viewed the plant primarily as a weed. Nowadays it is commercially cultivated for medicinal use, the oil is an excellent and easily assimilable source of Vitamin B and the plant has earned acclaim in the treatment of numerous complaints including PMS and menopausal problems, eczema, acne, asthma, migraine, metabolic disorders, arthritis and allergies.

Evening primroses will grow in sun in any reasonably deep soil. They are quite happy in drought and self-seed readily, or are easily propagated by seed sown in autumn in the position where they are to flower – some may flower in the first year but most will simply form rosettes that summer, to blossom the following year.

Paeonia lactiflora

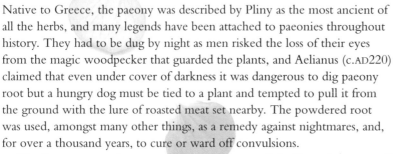

RANUNCULACEAE

paeony

Native to Greece, the paeony was described by Pliny as the most ancient of all the herbs, and many legends have been attached to paeonies throughout history. They had to be dug by night as men risked the loss of their eyes from the magic woodpecker that guarded the plants, and Aelianus (c.AD220) claimed that even under cover of darkness it was dangerous to dig paeony root but a hungry dog must be tied to a plant and tempted to pull it from the ground with the lure of roasted meat set nearby. The powdered root was used, amongst many other things, as a remedy against nightmares, and, for over a thousand years, to cure or ward off convulsions.

The first paeony to be grown in Britain was not *P. lactiflora*, the parent of the common herbaceous garden paeonies, but *P. mascula*. Native to Southern Europe, this male paeony arrived in Britain so early – probably around the 6th century – that it was thought to be native. It was immediately put to practical use and can still be found on the site of ancient monasteries where it was grown to cure men of epilepsy. *P. mascula* had impressive large flowers, around 5 inches (13cm) across, in pink, red or white.

P. officinalis, or the female paeony, was also a European native. It came into cultivation before 1548 but several centuries after *P. mascula*, and was chiefly recommended to cure women of fits. The reason for the split in gender has been lost to history. Gerard reported a double white variety in 1597, but it didn't appear in Britain until after his herbal was completed: the double white *P. officinalis* 'Alba Plena', is still in cultivation. By 1665, a "carnation-flowered" version was growing in Northern Europe, possibly the double crimson *P. officinalis* 'Rubra Plena' which is still grown. Apparently a red form streaked with white could also be found in the 17th century.

The Chinese were growing superior strains of *P. lactiflora* by the 11th century, but these didn't reach Britain until the end of the 18th century, arriving from Siberia and Mongolia where people added the roots to their soups and ground the seeds to make tea. By the 12th century, this species was sufficiently popular to warrant a monograph mentioning 39 varieties. So *P. lactiflora* was quite well developed long before it reached British shores in 1784 when the first herbaceous or Chinese paeony, a single white, arrived from Siberia. Other colours followed, but it wasn't until the 1820s that paeony breeding began in earnest in the West. Even the anemone-flowered types, which were touted as a modern breakthrough in 19th century Europe, probably originated almost a thousand years before, in 10th century China.

Chinese paeonies are long-lived plants; you can often find them lingering around old buildings decades after the house disappeared. They will tolerate poor soil, but they grow best in a moisture-retentive clay subsoil with light topsoil. They like to be kept moist but if they suffer from drought they will usually return the next season, even if less prolifically. They don't like being moved once established and may sulk for several seasons before grudgingly flowering again. Propagate paeonies by division – *P. lactiflora* hybrids are easily propagated, others may take more perseverance.

Recommended

P. lactiflora 'Edulis Superba': a tall and early blooming double pink cultivar dating back to the 1820s.

P. lactiflora 'Festiva Maxima': another early 19th century strain, white with crimson flecks.

P. lactiflora 'Sarah Bernhardt': a very popular prolific producer of large tissue pink blooms in midsummer. It was created in 1906.

P. suffruticosa (formerly *P. moutan*): the tree paeony, is intensely fragrant and bears huge blossoms. It was also cultivated in China from antiquity, but didn't arrive in Britain until 1787.

Penstemon

SCROPHULARIACEAE

penstemon

There are over 250 species of penstemon, native to North and Central America, yet this flower has always seemed to be more favoured in Europe, particularly in Britain, than in its homelands. Penstemon were first identified in 1748 by Dr John Mitchell, an English physician living in Virginia. *Penstemon hirsutus,* the pale blue chelone, was introduced to Britain from North America in 1758 and *P. laevigatus,* the penstemon chelone, was introduced in 1776.

One of the first penstemons to reach Europe at the end of the 18th century was *P. barbatus*, 3 foot (1m) tall plants bearing spikes of bright scarlet flowers in midsummer. *P. pinifolius* was another early introduction, short plants with miniature pine needle-like foliage produce orange-red trumpet flowers all summer. These and other species such as *P. hartwegii* thrive in poor soil, but *P. hartwegii* is more tender than most. *P. heterophyllus*, a sub-shrub brought from California in 1834, is the ancestor of all modern blue flowered cultivars.

Penstemon seed was voraciously collected by Victorian plant hunters, and the plants became hugely popular in England in the 19th century, with the first field trials of penstemon held in 1861 at the Royal Horticultural Society grounds at Chiswick. Penstemons have showy flower spikes of bell-shaped flowers, rather like foxgloves, and grow 1–4 feet (30–120cm) tall, depending on species and variety. Colours range from deep reds to blues and pale pinks, many white lobed. There was a rush to develop penstemons at the end of the 19th century, but unfortunately interest in the genus died down in the earlier part of the 20th century, largely due to the disruption of the wars, so few early varieties still exist. Now penstemons are back in favour, in British gardens anyway, and new cultivars are becoming available all the time, although it is hard to find the older species or hybrids.

There is a myth that most penstemons are tender. They like growing in a sunny position but there are penstemons suitable for almost every type of climate – they are grown in every state in North America, including Alaska, apart from Hawaii. Few penstemons object to cold, but the one thing they can't stand is having wet feet, which is the sure way to kill them. If your soil is heavy it is best to add grit or grow penstemons in a raised bed and don't mulch them as they prefer to have dry crowns. After flowering you should cut back spent flowers, otherwise prune plants lightly when new growth is appearing in mid spring. Some penstemons are short lived but it is worth growing the species from seed, shocking it in the refrigerator for a couple of weeks before planting.

Cultivars must be increased by taking cuttings from strong side shoots in August and placing them in a gritty mix of bulb compost, grit and sand for propagation. Overwinter cuttings in a cold frame before planting out in their final positions.

Recommended

P. campanulatus: popular in the 19th century, this species bears small purple flowers with white throats; it will flower all summer if continually dead headed.

P. diffusus/serrulatus: clusters of pale purple flowers in early autumn on $1^1/2$ foot (45cm) stems. It was introduced to England in 1826.

P. 'Garnet': a very reliable variety of another early introduction, *P. hartwegii,* bearing deep red flowers in late summer on 3 foot (1m) plants.

P. 'Countess of Dalkeith': a comparative newcomer, developed at the beginning of the 20th century, but immensely valuable in a border with its rich purple white-throated flowers growing to about $2^1/2$ feet (75cm).

P. 'Alice Hindley': the classic garden penstemon, growing up to 4 feet (120cm) and flowering profusely with pale mauve flowers.

Phlox

POLEMONIACEAE

phlox

Native to North America, phlox were most developed in Europe, particularly in England, during the 18th and 19th centuries. The sweetly scented *P. maculata* was the earliest arrival from eastern North America in 1640; it is a tidy upright (2–3 feet/60–90cm) plant with narrow dark green foliage and scented flowers on slightly mottled stems.

Despite their long history *P. maculata* 'Miss Lingard' is one of the oldest varieties currently in cultivation, developed in the mid 19th century. The sweetly scented border phlox *P. paniculata* was introduced to England in 1730 where its clusters of large scented flowers in white and shades of pinks and blues quickly became popular, good for height (up to 4 feet/120cm) and late colour as they flower in July and August. Many are quite striking, with a different coloured eye. *P. canadensis* also arrived in Europe in the 1730s, a lower growing phlox with pale lilac flowers with cut petals flowering from spring to midsummer, and the familiar spring blooming moss phlox arrived in England in 1745. Moss phlox *P. subulata* form generous mats of creeping needle-like foliage and flower in early summer, excellent for edging a dry bed. *P. stolonifera,* brought from North America in 1800 is another low growing species forming tidy mats which flower in late spring.

The worst problem with growing phlox is powdery mildew, but the older varieties seem much more resistant than modern hybrids. Space plants well in the border to minimise the risk, and plant in deep moist soil in full sun. Divide them every four or five years and thin out old shoots in spring to encourage strong blooming. Moss phlox prefer well-drained light soil and are quite drought resistant; they should be cut back hard after blooming and increased by division in early spring.

Recommended

P. maculata 'Miss Lingard': praised by the Victorian gardener William

Robinson in *The English Flower Garden* (1883). Flowers are pure white and leaves are a very dark green.

P. paniculata 'Graf Zeppelin': another popular 19th century variety; large white flowered heads have striking cherry coloured eyes.

P. paniculata 'Pheasant's Eye': a very old strong-growing variety with rose pink flowers with a deep mulberry pink eye.

Polemonium caeruleum

POLEMONIACEAE

Jacob's ladder

This European native is so named because the leaflets are arranged at right angles one to another, in ladder-like formation. *Polemonium caeruleum* was a favourite plant from the 16th century onwards, first firmly adopted into gardens under the name Greek valerian. Culpeper assigned all sorts of medicinal uses to Jacob's ladder including a cure for distempers, headaches, tremblings, palpitations of the heart and nervous complaints as well as epilepsy, providing a good excuse to invite it into the cottage garden, where it was common. The medicinal uses were largely forgotten so that Jacob's ladder was primarily valued for its purplish blue blossoms and their scent. It has open-faced mid-blue flowers with orange centres which cluster around the $1^1/2$–2 feet (45–60cm) stems from late spring to midsummer. By the 18th century, a version with striped flowers was reported, but seems to have vanished. The snowy white form *P. caeruleum album,* sometimes found as *P. alba,* was also available in the 18th century; it blooms rather later on taller stems. A variegated Jacob's ladder was once popular but could be propagated only by division; by 1887, it was already scarce. It has since disappeared.

Jacob's ladder likes to grow in full sun in moisture-retentive soil. It can be propagated by seed but it is easiest to increase plants by division in spring, or through basal cuttings.

Recommended

P. pauciflorum: came from Mexico at the end of the 19th century. Although it is less hardy than the native species it is an attractive lower growing plant with creamy apricot trumpet flowers and neat dark green foliage.

Polygonatum multiflorum

LILIACEAE

Solomon's seal, David's harp, Lady's lockets, ladder to heaven

This is an ancient plant, introduced into Britain in 1265. The name Solomon's seal was already in use by the early Middle Ages for this plant which produces drooping pearl-like flowers on arching flower stalks. Solomon was considered, in medieval minds, to be wise above all others, but also a conjuror and enchanter; his seal was the magic pentacle, and the plant may therefore get its name from its multijointed roots which, according to Gerard, "in some places resemble the marke of a seale". Other early commentators believe it was so named for its ability to seal wounds and heal broken bones.

Solomon's seal will grow in any cool and shaded spot but is an ideal plant for mosisture-retentive soil at the edges of woodland. It flowers in early summer with greenish white flowers above slender pointed leaves, growing 1-3 feet (30–90cm) with its clumps spreading rapidly when it is contented.

Recommended

P. 'Flore Pleno': a double form which produces prolific numbers of double bells, usually more white than green.

Primula

PRIMULACEAE

cowslip, primrose, bear's ear

Primula means first, and the plant is one of the first to flower, heralding the spring. Primroses and cowslips are native to much of Europe and widespread through Britain, particularly on limestone soil. Usually yellow in Northern Europe, in Eastern Europe the common primrose is replaced by *P. vulgaris sibthorpii* with predominantly pink to purple blooms, and in the Near East *P. vulgaris heterochroma* produces largely white or sometimes blue flowers. The Balearic Islands have their own native primrose *P. vulgaris balearica*, which is white and sweetly scented. *P. auricula*, also known as bear's ears or dusty miller, is a scented European alpine, brought to Northern Europe by Clusius in the 16th century.

The Japanese primrose *P. japonica* was a late introduction to European gardens, brought back from China by Robert Fortune in the mid 19th century, and other 19th century introductions include *P. rosea* from the Himalayas, and *P. sikkimensiis* from China or Northern India.

Primroses and cowslips were involved in many legends about fairies and elves, and praised in poetry and song. They were considered important healing flowers, used for everything from aching joints to paralysis as well as making cosmetics for refreshing or lightening the skin. Their medical uses date back to at least the ancient Greeks; one myth tells us that Paralisos, the son of the god Priapus and goddess Flora, died of grief because of the loss of his beloved, and his body was transformed by his parents into a primrose.

Primroses were one of the earliest plants to be brought from the wild into British gardens where they were common by the 15th century – added to salads, used for fritters and candied. For centuries cowslips *P. veris* were widely used in humble and grand kitchens, particularly for wines and desserts. Unusual floral structures were quite common in Tudor times; there were hose-in-hose versions, where the calyx looked like a petal to suggest one flower inside another; jack-in-the-greens where the sepals were replaced by miniature leaves so they resembled a ruff around the flower, and gally-gaskins where the calyx was inflated to resemble a kind of garter or a pair of pantaloons. Hose-in-hose variants can still be found today, although the other types seem to have disappeared. And cowslips, once so common, are nowadays protected plants, so make sure any plants you buy have not been dug from the wild. *P. elatior* is the native North European oxslip, a sadly rare near-relative to the cowslip but with larger paler flowers.

Polyanthus are crosses between *P. vulgaris* and *P. veris*, known to have occurred naturally in the 17th century, and later widely bred to bring a whole range of colours into the garden. During the 18th and 19th centuries primroses and polyanthus went in and out of fashion, and colour ranges were continually extended as new species were introduced.

P. auricula were arguably the most popular florists flowers (*see pp 73*) of the 19th century, when numerous forms were developed, in a wide variety of colours and markings. Many of these had a distinctive green frill but there were also numerous double and single lacy forms, and variations throughout the colour range including blues and greens, and plain or speckled forms some with distinctive coloured eyes. Some older forms can still be found.

All primulas prefer damp acid soil and shade and won't tolerate full sun or very dry conditions. Seeds require light to germinate so sow them on moist soil outside in autumn or in a cold frame in early spring. To keep cowslips flowering well year after year, divide plants every two or three years just after they have flowered. Primulas are easily propagated by division in autumn or spring.

Recommended

P. vulgaris 'Wanda': an old hybrid, widely grown in cottage gardens since the early 19th century, plants grow in tidy clumps producing masses of bright mauve flowers above dark leaves.

P. veris Gold Lace group: introduced in the mid 18th century, plants produce flowers laced with gold on each stem.

P. elatior 'Hose-in-hose': a rare variant of the native oxslip, where one flower appears to grow inside another.

P. auricula 'Argus': this 19th century auricula has rich ruby red flowers with darker shadings and a pale cream eye.

P. auricula 'Old Irish Scented': scented yellowish brown flowers have a cream centre and frilled edges.

Pulmonaria

BORAGINACEAE

lungwort, Jerusalem cowslip, soldiers and sailors

Lungwort has been grown in cottage gardens throughout their history; Gerard stated that it was planted almost everywhere in gardens in the 17th century, and pulmonarias still form the backbone of a garden in early spring. The leaves are long and rather lung-shaped and spotted in white, so early medicine based on the Doctrine of Signatures compared the leaves to lungs and so considered them to be suitable to cure lung problems. It was also thought that drops of the Virgin's milk or the Virgin's tears had fallen on the leaves and spotted them.

Lungworts flower in early spring, pink then violet-blue flowers appearing before the leaves which are spotted with silvery white blotches of varying sizes. Although they will grow in the sun as long as the soil is moist they fare best and are at their most striking in dappled shade where their spotted foliage appears more prominent. Cut the flower stems to the ground after blooming for the best foliage. They spread easily and can be propagated by division in the autumn.

Recommended

P. officinalis: the original common lungwort is now increasingly rare. It produces numerous pink and blue flowers over silver spotted leaves. Unlike modern cultivars, this comes true from seed, and it will grow in any soil as long as it is in partial shade.

P. saccharata (syn *argentea*) has grown in Britain since the 17th century, with very silvery leaves, happy in sun or partial shade.

P. angustifolia azurea: blue lungwort is another old wild pulmonaria in popular cultivation; small intensely blue flowers appear before narrow dark green leaves with minimal spotting.

P. saccharata 'Mrs Moon': although this was only introduced earlier this century, it is worth growing for its heavily spotted, almost silver foliage.

Ranunculus

RANUNCULACEAE

fair maids of France, crowfoot, gold cup, bachelor's buttons

Many types of ranunculus have been grown in European gardens for at least five centuries. Unlike the native meadow buttercup, *R. acris*, garden forms are not invasive and are often excellent for cutting as well as making good border fillers. *R. ficaria*, the lesser celandine, comes in many forms to brighten up shady places in spring.

The attractive double white flowers of *R. aconitifolius*, fair maids of France, became popular in British gardens soon after they were brought from the Alps with Huguenot emigrants fleeing from France in 1572. Gerard called it "double white crowfoot", and Parkinson "double mountain crowfoot". A surprising use for crowfoot was borrowed from Apuleius (c.200) by Gerard: "if it be hanged in a linnen cloath about the necke of him that is lunaticke at the wain of the moon when the sign shall be in the first degree of Taurus or Scorpio, then he shall forthwith be cured".

William Robinson, who campaigned vigorously for cottage garden plants, wrote in 1870 that the small flowers of the double white ranunculus "are so white and neat and pretty and double that they resemble miniature double white camellias."

All crowfoots need cool moist soil and prefer shade. Lift plants every third year and divide them in autumn – their tuberous roots tend to knit together so you may have to cut them apart, but this won't hurt the plants.

Recommended

R. acris flore pleno: these double golden buttercups on 2 foot (60cm) almost leafless stems have been grown in gardens since the 16th century.

R. ficaria alba: a rare native celandine with starry pure white flowers.

Rosa

ROSACEAE

roses

Roses have existed since antiquity, praised by each civilisation in turn. The Romans dedicated the rose to the goddess of love Venus, and to Bacchus the god of wine; no banquet was complete without rose petals strewn over couches, tables and floors; they floated on the surface of wine; garlands of roses decorated halls and were worn round necks and on heads. As well as all its sensual delights, when a garland of roses was hung in a dining hall or around a person's neck it had the added meaning that any word uttered was 'sub rosa' – under the rose – and should therefore not be repeated outside the hall or out of the present company. One extraordinary report stated that Nero spent four million sesterces for roses at a single banquet (a sesterce was a brass coin that was apparently equal in value to four donkeys). During the days of Roman decadence the demand for roses was so great that Roman colonies, including Egypt, grew roses in large numbers for export to Rome.

The rose was originally valued in early European gardens as a medicinal herb. Walafrid Strabo, a 9th century German monk-gardener and writer of Hortulus, a celebrated poem on gardening, wrote that oil of roses could be used to cure nearly any ailment. He was probably referring to *R. gallica*. Native from France to Persia, *R. gallica* is thought to have been known as early as the 12th century BC, and said to have been the rose of the Persian Magi and the Medean fire-worshippers. *R. gallica* was probably the red rose of the Greeks, said to have grown out of the blood of Adonis.

R. gallica officinalis is also known as the apothecary's rose, now the sole source of petals recommended for apothecary purposes. This semi-double red flowering rose was adopted as the symbol of the House of Lancaster in the Wars of the Roses, taken by Edmund (the first Earl of Lancaster) as his emblem in 1277. *R. alba* was adopted by his opponents as the white rose of York. *R. alba* is a very old race of rather upright summer flowering roses which are well scented and disease-resistant, producing an abundance of pale blossoms on vigorous plants with greyish foliage. Tudor women once used rose water from *R. alba* as a cosmetic, bags full of rose petals to ensure a good night's sleep, and made a soothing eye salve from them.

Musk roses *R. moschata*, native to southern Europe, Persia and the Himalayas, were introduced to Britain in 1590. They have always been prized for their heavy fragrance, but the damask roses are perhaps the most heavily scented of all roses. The autumn damask rose, *R. bifera,* is very ancient, it was apparently growing on the Greek island of Samos in the 10th century BC. It was used in the cult of Aphrodite and is thought to have been the rose grown in the garden of King Midas. *R. bifera* was cultivated at Pompeii, and used by the Arabs for making rose water. It flowers in summer and again in autumn.

R. gallica was one of the original parents of the summer damask rose, *R. damascena* (*R.* x *damascena*), a hybrid so ancient that it was portrayed in about 2000BC on Minoan-Cretan wall paintings near the Palace of Knossos. *R. damascena* is said to have been brought from Damascus to Europe by a Crusader, and was certainly popular in England by the 16th century – Queen Elizabeth I was said to use damask scent.

By the 17th century roses were becoming widely grown, and cabbage roses *R. centifolia* and their near relatives the moss roses began to evolve in many gardens. China roses *R. chinensis* are repeat-flowering types which blossom all season, and took Europe by storm when they were introduced in the mid-18th century. Scotch roses, *R. spinosissima* (*pimpinellifolia*) followed hard on their heels, and by the 19th century rose breeding was very well developed with many hundreds of different roses in cultivation, including the useful compact repeat flowering Portland roses which were followed by Bourbon roses in the mid 19th century – their generous flowers, scent and repeat-flowering characteristics were very popular in Victorian times.

Hybrid perpetuals also emerged in the mid 19th century and evolved to supersede the Bourbons as the most popular Victorian roses. They have very varied forms, but many are large and blowsy and by the end of the 19th century there was a backlash against the buxom blooms Victorian gardeners loved, and a desire to return to simpler forms and shapes. Thanks largely to the influence of William Robinson and Gertrude Jekyll species and shrub roses again became more popular, along with old varieties of small flowered ramblers and climbers. *R. rugosa*, rugosa roses, also became more widely grown at the turn of the century, forming excellent shrubs and decorative hedges with scented blooms and good autumn fruit.

Although the qualities of old-fashioned roses are now once again recognised by many gardeners, there have been many losses. For example, in the early 19th century, the Empress Josephine was growing 2,000 cultivars of *R. gallica* in her gardens at Malmaison. Of these, only about 100 can now be found.

Roses vary enormously and so have many different planting requirements, depending on type and variety; some are compact, some hugely rampant; some climb tidily while others ramble everywhere; some are upright, others procumbent – there are roses for every garden. A general rule is to prepare soil well in advance of planting, digging deeply and adding quantities of organic material plus bonemeal to help roots get established; then dig a hole large enough to accommodate all the roots without cramping them, and firm the soil well around the rose, topdressing with bonemeal. You can prune old-fashioned roses pretty much to your own taste but at the end of their first year it is wise to prune most types, just the once, to within 6 inches (15cm) of the ground. This starts off growth from the base and avoids the plants becoming leggy. Roses with a long flowering season get untidy and leggy more quickly than those with a shorter season, so need to be pruned fairly hard and any weak growth removed, but it really depends on how you want the rose to grow. It is hard irrevocably to damage a rose by hard pruning at the end of winter, but they can get untidy if you leave them too long without attention.

Recommended

Everyone has favourite types of roses, so recommendation is very much a matter of personal taste. Hundreds of old roses are available from specialist suppliers throughout Europe. Some modern roses, such as David Austin's "English roses", also have all the best characteristics of old-fashioned types, but have greatly increased resistance to mildew and blackspot.

R. alba maxima: the Jacobite rose or White rose of York, a 16th century variety which produces masses of white flowers with creamy tinted centres on vigorous plants growing to about 6 feet (180cm). Leaves are a dense green and the autumn fruit is attractive.

R. alba 'Cuisse de Nymphe'/'Maiden's Blush': this rose was grown before the 15th century; it has double soft pale pink flowers with a very strong sweet scent, and greyish leaves. It reaches about 6 feet (180cm).

R. damascena 'Kazanlik' ('Trigintipetala'): this vigorous ancient rose has soft warm pink blossoms with incredible scent. It forms a shrub about 5 feet (150cm) tall.

R. damascena 'Blush Damask': a smaller shrub rose, no taller than 4 feet (120cm), produces small pale pink blossoms with deep pink centres and incredible scent.

R. gallica versicolor 'Rosa Mundi': a popular bushy rose, widely grown in cottage gardens, dates back to the 12th century, and is believed to be named after fair Rosamund, mistress of Henry II. Semi-double blossoms have splashes of pink and white on a crimson background; however 'Rosa Mundi' may tend to revert to crimson.

R centifolia: the species cabbage rose has large bright pink double blooms on long stems. It is highly scented and was cultivated in the Middle Ages.

R. 'Common Moss': one of the oldest moss roses, much grown before 1700, with clear pink blossoms which are deliciously fragrant.

R. 'Cécile Brunner': not one of the oldest China roses, but one of the most popular, this late 19th century rose is very free flowering, producing masses of delicately scented small soft pink blooms over a long period. The shrubby form is fairly low growing, and a reliable climbing form is also available.

Saponaria

CARYOPHYLLACEEAE

soapwort, fuller's herb, bouncing Bet, farewell summer

The popular widespread European native *Saponaria officinalis* was a common cottage garden plant, probably first invited in from the wild for practical purposes as its leaves lather easily to make a soft soap. Crush a few soapwort leaves between your fingers and you will discover how easily it lathers. It was used for centuries to wash delicate fabrics, and some museum textile curators today still use soapwort for cleaning fragile old cloth and tapestries. Flowers are usually pale pink but white or darker pink forms are also found; all are sweetly scented and flower for a long time from midsummer on when most plants are ending their season. They thrive in a sunny position in most soils but some gardeners can find them invasive as their roots run about – plant soapwort somewhere where it has room to wander; it is easiest to propagate by division after flowering.

Recommended

S. officinalis plena alba: branching clusters of white budded double white flowers age to pale pink. This plant spreads as vigorously as the single form.

Valeriana officinalis

VALERIANACEAE

valerian, garden heliotrope, all heal

This common British native grows wild as a weed in some parts, spreading rampantly in moist wasteground and in neglected gardens. It is also a valuable cottage garden plant, its deep pink or white flowers blooming right through late summer. Valerian flowers have a marked scent, and the roots are even more pungent, hence the name "phu" used by Dioscorides for all plants with an offensive smell and still attached to some varieties of valerian.

Valerian tea is commonly drunk throughout Europe and has been used for many centuries as a relaxant and to induce sleep. For centuries country-women used to gather the roots to sell to druggists, and valerian still has a medicinal place in the *British Pharmacopeia*. It makes a bright statement in the garden, through its flowers or the attractive foliage of some varieties.

Recommended

V. phu aurea: golden valerian moved from Eastern to Northern Europe in 1597. Athough the small flowers are rather insignificant, this form has gleaming golden foliage in spring, fading in the heat of summer.

Verbascum

SCROPHULARIACEAE

mullein

Verbascum appeared in mediaeval monastery gardens, its tall downy spikes used as candle-wicks. The native verbascum has tall spikes of yellow flowers and large downy greyish leaves, but the striking purple flowered species *V. phoenicum* arrived from Asia in 1796. *V. chaixii* from southern Europe arrived at around the same time, a nettle-leaved mullein with pale yellow flowers with different coloured eyes. Numerous hybrids then followed, in increasingly varied colour combinations. You can now find verbascum in almost every pastel shade you could think of.

Verbascums are easy to grow on light dry soils in sunny situations. Each flower lasts a disappointingly short time but the plants self-seed copiously so a display can continue for several months. Sow seed in autumn where plants are to flower, or sow in pots in a cold frame in early spring and plant out. Once established, the surest way to propagate plants is by division, and the only way to make sure a colour will come true.

Viola

VIOLACEAE

viola, heartsease, garden pansy

The viola family encompasses more than 400 species including violas, garden pansies and violets. The boundaries between them all were blurred by Victorian plant breeders who worked at hybridising the perennial garden viola.

Four native European violas are the ancestors of most of today's cultivated violas and pansies: the annual *V. tricolor* which is the original heartsease of early physic gardens – used to stimulate the nervous system and cleanse the blood – and the perennials *V. cornuta* from the Pyrenees, *V. lutea* from Southern Europe, and *V. altaica* from the eastern Mediterranean and Russia.

Modern garden pansies were originally bred from *V. tricolor* and *V. lutea*, and widely developed during the 1820s and 1830s; by 1835 over 400 named garden pansies existed in England alone. Pansy development was followed by work on hybridising violas, crossing the garden pansy with other viola species, and the most fragrant viola cultivars, bred from *V. odorata*, became very popular in Victorian gardens.

The original *V. cornuta* has violet-blue flowers; the species and its cultivars grow to form large carpets of colour, very effective as underplanting in a border and more tolerant of hot and dry conditions than most violas which prefer semi-shade and moisture-retentive soil. They flower from early summer right through to autumn; cut them back when they become straggly to encourage new growth. The only way reliably to propagate most named violas is by layering young shoots in spring or dividing plants in autumn. However a few do come true from seed, such as the small-flowered 'Bowles Black', a cultivar of *V. tricolor*.

Recommended

V. 'Bowles Black': grown by E. A. Bowles in his famous 19th century garden, this is a useful and attractive viola, forming dark mats of tiny flowers, ideal for underplanting or at the front of a border.

V. 'Irish Molly': an early Victorian cultivar with reddish brown flowers shadowed with lime green and yellow and a very dark centre. Its growing habit is less tidy and compact than many, but ideal for underplanting in a shady border.

V. 'Jackanapes': named after Gertrude Jekyll's pet monkey. Bright yellow and rusty red flowers bloom from spring to midsummer.

V. 'Maggie Mott': a very fragrant late 19th century viola. Its silvery mauve flowers with a cream centre make a striking display all summer.

ANNUALS

Amaranthus

AMARANTHACEAE

love-lies-bleeding

Native to Peru, Africa and India, *Amaranthus caudatus* was described as a countrywoman's flower by Thomas Tusser in the 16th century, and called the "great purple flower-gentle" by Gerard and Parkinson. The botanical name, amaranthus, means "never waxing old", referring to the plant's everlasting qualities.

Amaranth produces dramatic drooping crimson tassels that are highly decorative. It has been popular for centuries, becoming particularly popular in the early 19th century, and then in Victorian gardens.

A later introduction *A. hypochondriacus* arrived in Britain from Virginia in 1684. Native to the southern United States, Mexico, India and China, Prince's feather (as it was quickly nicknamed) boasts tall, upright, crimson plumes and was originally grown as a food crop for its nutritious seeds.

Amaranths love sunny weather but wilt easily when conditions are dry. They are often grown on windowsills or in boxes as well as in the border.

Antirrhinum

SCROPHULARIACEAE

snapdragon

The original purple-flowering *Antirrhinum majus*, native to southwestern Europe and the Mediterranean, was probably brought to Britain with the Romans. They were certainly popular by the 16th century, although they blossomed in only five different colours: purple, white, pink, red with yellow throat or red with yellow veins. They were also much taller than more recent varieties, at about 3 feet (90cm) tall. Snapdragons are an exception to the general rule that flowers tend to lose their scent during hybridisation and development. The first scented versions only appeared in the mid 1900s.

The colour range increased from the early 19th century and by the 1850s the first striped snapdragons appeared, debuting as *A. hendersonii*. They were developed further for bedding use and the dwarf 'Tom Thumb' series was popular in the 1880s, along with double snapdragons. Those double hybrids were difficult to propagate and soon disappeared from the scene. Some older hybrids were also prone to rust.

Snapdragons can be treated as biennials. The seed should be started early (February is not too soon) to see flowers by midsummer. They prefer full sun and fertile well-drained soil. If you deadhead them as soon as the seed-buttons begin to form they may flower on the side shoots.

Calendula officinalis

ASTERACEAE

pot marigold

Although ancient identification is notoriously uncertain, the "gold flower" of ancient Greece is often considered to be calendula. If this is the case, calendula would be the flower that Theophrastus, in the 3rd century BC, mentioned for a variety of ailments of the head. The name calendula comes from the Roman *calends* meaning the first day of the month, as it was claimed these flowers were in bloom on every *calends* throughout the year; this could be possible in a southern Mediterranean climate. They were cultivated very early on as ornaments and as medicinal herbs, particularly used for bites and stings.

Native throughout Southern Europe, marigolds were widely grown in British gardens by the 15th century, and probably centuries before, a staple ingredient of every cottage and kitchen garden. The single flowered types were traditionally used as kitchen and medicinal herbs, and the doubles, known since at least the 16th century, were grown in flower beds. Marigold was a common flavouring, a "sweet herb" used for centuries in puddings, pottages and possets (a popular Tudor milk and herb based drink to which beer or ale was added).

Gerard described large double marigolds "like pure gold", and hen-and-chicken forms were apparently common in the 16th and 17th centuries. If you grow pot marigolds for long enough, such sports sometimes still occur among double flowered types. The flowerheads of calendula (like most of the daisy family) face the sun, and Charles I of England wrote before his execution, "The marigold observes the sun, More than my subjects me have done."

Marigolds grow to 2 feet (60cm) in the wild in Southern Europe, with pale yellow to dark orange blooms up to 4 inches (10cm) across, many with darker centres. Many late 19th and early 20th century cultivars have been bred to boast very dark centres.

Sow marigolds in autumn or spring in any reasonable soil, in sun or dappled shade, covering seeds with a scattering of soil as they need dark to germinate. Sow a second time in early summer for late blooming marigolds, providing attractive bright autumn colour.

Recommended

C. 'Orange King': a vigorous late 19 century cultivar with large double orange flowers and green or dark centres, particularly striking for autumn colour.

Centaurea cyanus

COMPOSITAE

cornflower, bluebottle, bachelor's buttons

The Egyptian boy king Tutankhamen was buried *c.*1340BC with a funerary wreath around his head made of cornflowers, olive leaves and waterlily petals. We know that beautiful deep blue cornflowers have grown for many centuries, throughout Europe and into Asia. Their Latin name *Centaurea cyanus* comes from the mythical centaur who reputedly healed himself with cornflowers after he was wounded by an arrow poisoned with the blood of Hydra. In later centuries the Doctrine of Signatures suggested that they be used to ease eye complaints – comparing the blue of the flowers with the blue of people's eyes. The practice of using cornflowers as eye salve persisted for many centuries.

Cornflowers have wiry silver leaved stems growing up to 3 feet (1m) tall with many fringed deep blue brushlike flowers. They were once so common in cornfields that the farmers called them "hurtsickles" as their stems could (apparently) blunt a sickle. They were also called bluebottles because of their resemblance to little blue pouches of ink, and people used to make a blue ink from the petals.

Once very common in Northern European arable fields, and self-seeding in nearly every rural garden, cornflowers are sadly one of the catastrophes of 20th century farming methods and they are now a very rare sight in the wild, although they remain a popular annual, particularly with children as they are easy and rewarding to grow.

Cornflower's other common name of bachelor's buttons may refer to their popularity as buttonhole flowers in Victorian times, as their stems are very resilient and the blooms keep fresh well even when cut, but it is more likely to refer to their shaggy-headed habit. It is said that they resemble traditional bachelor's buttons which were made from small pieces of cloth stitched on top of one another.

Sow seeds in well-drained soil in autumn or early spring for continuous blossoming right into the autumn.

Consolida

RANUNCULACEAE

larkspur

Formerly known as *Delphinium ajacus* and currently classified as *Consolida ambigua*, larkspur was introduced to Britain from its native Mediterranean some time before the middle of the 16th century and was soon naturalised, growing as a weed in cornfields. Although Fuchs chose a single larkspur to illustrate in his herbal of 1545, both Parkinson and Gerard were familiar with the double version, having stems surrounded in little mops of many petals. Larkspurs are often mentioned in the same breath as delphiniums, which have similar characteristics but are perennial and biennial while larkspur perishes promptly after flowering.

Larkspur may once have been applied as a wound herb, and in the 17th century the juice of the flower was believed to strengthen eyesight, while the poisonous seed was used as an insecticide, particularly as a cure for head-lice. Commonly grown in gardens throughout the 17th and 18th centuries, larkspur plants used to be up to 2 feet (60cm) tall but shorter hybrids are more common today.

Larkspur prefers fairly light but fertile soil and likes to grow in full sun in a group. It self-sows prolifically but is easily uprooted if it ends up where it is not wanted. Sow seed directly onto well-drained soil in early summer.

Convolvulus tricolor (Ipomoea tricolor)

CONVOLVULACEAE

three coloured morning glory

Convolvulus is a name which strikes terror into most gardeners, with visions of perennial bindweed *Convolvulus arvensis* gradually trying to encroach and rampage through every border and vegetable plot, requiring endless patience to eradicate it. When *C. tricolor* arrived in Britain from Spain in 1621, it suffered at first from guilt by association, even though it is a low growing sprawling annual with much larger flowers than its relative; it brightens a summer bed, then disappears. However, it was in the list of plants growing in John Tradescant's garden at Lambeth, and later offered for sale in William Lucas' 1677 catalogue.

Short-lived flowers are produced all summer long, similar to bindweeds or morning glories (ipomoea); they are traditionally blue with a white throat and yellow eye, but other colour forms can often be found.

Cosmos bipinnatus

ASTERACEAE

Mexican aster

This striking annual is native to Mexico and Central America, popular in North America since the beginning of the 19th century, but more of a recent comer to Europe. Feathery foliage complements large daisy-like flowers resembling single dahlias, traditionally pale pink, growing on tall stems. They make an attractive plant for the back of the border, blooming at the end of summer into autumn.

In 1838 the entrepreneurial New York garden sundries and seed supplier Grant Thorburn was offering his customers 6 feet (180cm) tall "late Cosmos", and there was little development of the species through the 19th century, but the disadvantage of traditional varieties of cosmos is their late blooming. So in the early 20th century new earlier flowering strains of cosmos were developed.

Seed should be sown in warm soil, and barely covered. Plants seem to fare best in poorer soils, in sun or dappled shade. The flowers self-seed profusely, but they almost always revert to the most vigorous pale pink form so select seed and grow in isolation to keep the colours true. The white forms are least vigorous, so it is particularly important to save seed from them.

Helianthus annuus

COMPOSITAE

sunflower

Native to the southern states of Northern America, sunflowers must have travelled into South America in very early days as sunflowers were a staple Inca crop, grown for the oil and the seeds. The Spanish took sunflowers back to Spain in the 16th century, and they were first mentioned in English in 1577 in *Joyfull News out of the Newfounde Worlde*, a translation of an earlier work by the Spanish botanist Monardes. Gerard was growing sunflowers in his garden at Holborn in 1596. He said that he ate the flowerbuds like globe artichokes "surpassing the Artichoke far in procuring bodily lust."

Despite their provenance, sunflowers were not widely used as an oil crop until the 20th century, but they are now seen as primarily agricultural throughout Southern Europe, and in Britain they are seen more as a garden curiosity or children's plant than as worthwhile flowers in their own right. Yet some forms are very striking; Northern American varieties range from red to pale yellow, and include many very dark forms – also grown in Russia for centuries – and those with heads up to 18 inches (40cm) across.

Sunflowers are incredibly easy to sow, just bury the large seeds about half an inch (1cm) below ground in a sunny position. Gerard referred to a sunflower in the Royal Garden in Madrid which reached 24 feet (8m) but this could be a slight exaggeration.

Heliotropium

BORAGINACEAE

heliotrope, cherry pie

Most species of heliotrope are found in South America and the one originally grown in gardens was *Heliotropium peruviana*, honouring its place of origin. It was introduced by Joseph de Jussieu into France's Jardin du Roi in Paris in 1757. From there it travelled to Britain where the headily fragrant flower became instantly popular and Philip Miller had already been growing it for a few years in the Chelsea Physic Garden when it was listed there in

1768. The name recalls the way the flower turns to face the sun – in Greek, *helio*s means sun and *trope* means to turn. It was also once commonly called turnsole for the same reason.

The first heliotropes were tall and untidy plants with fragrant bluish flowers. *H. corymbosum*, which arrived in Europe in 1800 was more compact with better coloured flowers but precious little fragrance. When these two forms were hybridised they produced fragrant and well coloured forms. Heliotrope was extremely popular at the end of the 19th century when many cultivars were produced with varying habits, grown as bedding plants then sheltered in greenhouses as soon as the first chill threatened. Later, specific winter-flowering varieties, such as the snowy-hued *H.* 'White Lady' (still in cultivation under the name *H. arborescens* 'Alba') were developed for the conservatory. Nineteenth century books described heliotropes with golden variegated leaves as well as double flowers in shades ranging from lilac to deep purple. Few catalogues now offer anything other than *H. arborescens*. Although cultivars were still popular until the middle of the 20th century, most probably disappeared with the Second World War when many plants that had to be propagated vegetatively and overwintered in heat were lost.

H. arborescens forms compact fragrant cushions of deep purple flowers. Plants have to be grown from cuttings and overwintered in a frost-free place as plants grown from seed rarely have any fragrance. Heliotrope is very tender and should be the last plant put out in spring and the first to be taken in at the end of summer. It also tends to attract white fly, red spider mite and aphids so it is a good idea to plant insect-repellant plants such as African marigolds *Tagetes erecta* not far away.

Iberis umbellata

CRUCIFERAE

candytuft

Iberis umbellata was first recorded by Gerard at the end of the 16th century, when he received plants from Candy, the old name for Crete. In 1629 Parkinson called the plant "Spanish tufts", receiving his plants from Iberia (the old name for Spain).

Although candytuft is not mentioned in early herbals, it was commonly known as sciatica weed in the 18th century, and since its introduction it has been a universal cottage garden plant, although never fashionable in sophisticated gardens.

Candytuft is an ideal child's plant as the seeds germinate quickly, grow fast, flower quickly and fade away soon, all before interest is lost! White, pink and red cultivars exist, but the oldest forms were always white or very pale pink. Sow seeds in a sunny place in soil that is not too rich.

Impatiens balsamina

BALSAMINACEAE

balsam, touch-me-not

An Asian native, this plant had arrived in Britain by 1596 but was recorded earlier in Germany where Fuchs *Herbal* of 1542 referred to it as a "recent introduction planted already in many gardens".

In the 17th and 18th centuries it was the custom to sow seeds of this and other heat-loving introductions on "hot beds", piles of fresh manure covered by a layer of soil to keep the heat rising. The earliest plants grown in Britain were single with purplish pink flowers but a white flowered form was recorded growing as early as 1620, and Philip Miller was growing red, white and striped singles and doubles at the Chelsea Physic Garden in 1768. These double balsams were very popular in the 18th century, called camellia balsams because the ideal blossoms resembled camellias. Unfortunately the seed was often unreliable.

It takes patience to grown balsams from seed, those started indoors in March will not blossom until the end of July, and they must be kept well-watered and shaded. Some camellia flowered types are still available, but balsams aren't as popular as they used to be.

I. walleriana, the busy Lizzie, came from Zanzibar in 1896 and was little grown until the 1950s. *I. noli-tangere*, touch-me-not, has been a rampant and therefore little-loved weed in Britain for centuries.

Lobularia maritima

CRUCIFERAE

sweet alyssum, sweet Alison

Sweet alyssum has gone through several name changes so it is impossible to know whether the flower we grow today is the same plant that was, according to Gerard, once used to cure the bite of a mad dog. However, it is fairly certain that it is native to Southern Europe and was included in gardens dating back to the 16th century.

By 1900, sweet alyssum was one of the commonest annuals, grown in gardens great and small for its neat little mounds of white honey-scented blossoms. Advertised for its qualities in attracting bees, the original sweet alyssum was slightly taller than the current more compact version. The modern pink version is neither so attractive as the old nor very useful as the colour is harsh and difficult to blend with other old-fashioned plants.

Sweet alyssum is extremely easy to grow and useful as edging or in windowboxes and summer tubs where it tolerates drought, rain or beating sun and requires virtually no attention. Seeds germinate very easily.

Matthiola incana

CRUCIFERAE

stocks, Brompton stocks

Stocks were probably brought from Southern Europe into England by the Normans; both perennial and annual stocks were well established by the 16th century. William Turner grew a purple and single white form in 1548 and by 1597 Gerard had added pink and striped forms as well as doubles. An unbranched biennial strain was developed at the end of the 17th century by the nurserymen London and Wise, and it came to be called Brompton stock after their nursery.

Brompton stocks are very worthwhile fragrant bedding plants, standing 1-2 feet (30–60cm) tall with soft, hoary gray leaves crowned by 8-10 inch (20–25cm) spires of dense fragrant blossoms in shades of pinks and blues, singles and doubles. Seeds sown in summer may flower the following spring, and it is possible to sow throughout the year for a display from spring through to late summer. Double forms are sterile but plants raised from garden-sown seed produce a high proportion of doubles, so stocks were often sown in the kitchen garden from where the doubles could be transplanted. All stocks have a wonderful scent which has diminished little through time. They thrive in deep, moderately rich soil and don't like to dry out.

Matthiola incana var. *annua* is a true annual used for summer display; they are also known as ten week stocks as this is said to be the length of time it takes from sowing to flowering. They fade rapidly, so in order to prolong their flowering it helps to pinch out the centre stalk and deadhead as soon as a flowerhead opens halfway – the harvested flower spire will keep quite a while in a vase. Stocks are usually supplied in mixed colours so you may need to save selected seed and grow your own if you seek certain shades, but you will need to segregate your preferred coloured varieties early on to have the best chance of collecting seeds for a specific colour.

Mirabilis jalapa

NYCTAGINACEAE

marvel of Peru, four o'clock

Some good plants slip out of fashion for no apparent reason, and marvel of Peru is a good example. Native to Peru, *Mirabilis jalapa* was introduced into Britain by the end of the 16th century, via Spain. Linnaeus classified it as *jalapa* because he thought it was the source of the drug jalap, but it was later found that he was mistaken. Although it can be grown as a tender perennial in some parts of the world, in Northern Europe it is an annual.

Quickly reaching 3 feet (1m) in diameter, the plant produces numerous terminal heads of fluted flowers, each of which unfolds in late afternoon, giving off a citrusy smell, remaining open through the night but over by the following morning. Sixteenth and 17th century gardeners adored this plant for its large number of flower colours, including white, rose, magenta, butter yellow, striped, spotted and variegated. Flowers of different colours can appear on one plant, or a single flower can even have petals of different colours. In warmer countries these colour variations don't seem so marked, so they may be caused by the lower temperatures the plant experiences when growing in Northern Europe.

Marvel of Peru is a good choice for a child's garden, or for a cold conservatory, but it was once equally appealing to cottage gardeners. It gradually fell out of favour in the 20th century. *M. jalapa* is a garden escape in North America where it can often be found in deserted gardens or derelict buildings. Fortunately, few of the once-popular varieties have disappeared and an old Spanish variety called 'Don Pedros', with a large proportion of striped and spotted flowers, is commercially available.

Marvel of Peru makes tubers which can be dug after the first frost and stored during the winter, but it is easiest to grow from rapidly germinating seeds which should be sown in gentle heat in early spring. Seed grown plants are fully capable of reaching impressive proportions and blooming freely in one growing season. The plants tolerate poor soil, and will grow in partial shade though they prefer a sunny spot.

Nicotiana sylvestris

SOLANACEAE

flowering tobacco

Nicotiana was named for Jean Nicot (1530–1600), the consul from the King of France to Portugal who first obtained tobacco from a Belgian merchant in 1560 and presented it, first to the court of Portugal and then, back in France, to Queen Catherine de Medici. The tobacco he brought back was *Nicotiana tabacum*, native to northeast Argentina and Bolivia, and the source of smoking tobacco, grown by Native Americans for that purpose long before Europeans arrived on the continent. It was introduced into Britain by Sir Walter Raleigh in 1586, prohibited by several kings, and wasn't widely grown in gardens.

Ornamental flowering tobacco has a different origin. *N. alata*, native to northeast Argentina and Southern Brazil, wasn't much grown in gardens until the end of the 19th century, although it was undoubtedly discovered earlier. The cream-coloured blossoms crown stems whch typically vary from 3–6 feet (1-2m) tall, releasing a strong perfume in the evenings. Victorian gardeners particularly welcomed nicotiana as it perfectly fitted into their night-scented gardens, popular so ladies could walk into the garden in the evening when all danger of being burnt by the sun was long past. The flowers not only release a wonderful scent, they also seem to glow at dusk, attracting their pollinators. Like *N. tabacum*, their leaves can be used to deter aphids as they have insecticidal properties.

N. sylvestris, with plump umbels of long pure white, tubular blossoms, is of comparatively recent vintage, arriving in cultivation from Argentina in 1899. Seed savers have introduced a strain of *N. alata* from Russia with purple, white, salmon, fuchsia, pink and rust-coloured blossoms, increasing the colour range drastically while preserving the perfume.

Flowering tobacco is easy to grow in any well-drained soil; although plants flower for longest in long hot and dry summers they also thrive in an average English summer as long as it is not too persistently wet.

Nigella damascena

RANUNCULACEAE

love-in-a-mist

Nigella is one of the best-loved cottage garden annuals, its feathery round blue flowers blooming throughout the summer and reseeding themselves vigorously for following years. Native to Southern Europe and Northern Africa and grown in gardens before 1548, the botanical name comes from *niger*, referring to the very ornamental black seed pods. Those seed pods found multiple uses through history, and were apparently crushed to make one of many cures to banish freckles in the 16th century.

The original *N. damascena* stood about 2 feet (60cm) tall with a delightful mist of frilly leaves that matched the floral bracts, but dwarf versions are nowadays more common, in white and pinks as well as blues. The seed pods last indefinitely in dried arrangements. The end of the 16th century brought double forms and whites were also available at that time.

Love-in-a-mist doesn't need much encouragement once established; it reseeds itself rampantly and most gardeners will have to weed out some seedlings after a year or two, but this is no great chore as they are easy to remove if they spread too vigorously. They prefer fairly loose well-drained soil to get started, and it is best to sow seed in autumn just below the soil surface, where it survives the worst winters. They are particularly attractive scattered in clumps through a border which contains any white daisy-like flowers, but it is easiest just to let them grow anywhere and pull up the ones you don't want.

Papaver

PAPAVERACEAE

poppy, opium poppy, lettuce poppy, corn poppy

At least 50 species of annual and perennial poppies are native to Europe, and another 100 grow throughout the Northern Hemisphere and in California. *Papaver somnifera*, the opium poppy or lettuce poppy was probably introduced into Britain from Southern Europe by the Romans. Lettuce poppies were widely grown in medieval monastic and early cottage gardens, although it was not until 1794 that they were first grown agriculturally in Britain for extracting opium (for medicinal use) by making incisions in the poppies' large seedpods. Poppies have often been seen as symbols of fertility because of these large seedpods; apparently a single plump pod can hold as many as 32,000 seeds – Linnaeus is alleged to have counted them! Opium poppies come in shades of lilac, pink, purple or white, singles and doubles, most with a telltale darkened spot in their centre. Gerard mentioned white, purple, red, purple streaked and scarlet flowers.

P. rhoeas, the corn poppy, is another ancient species that grows wild throughout Europe as well as Africa and Asia. These 1–3 feet (30–90cm) tall plants with their ephemeral red blossoms and greyish, tooth-edged leaves were once a common sight on arable land and also long cultivated in gardens. Modern strains of *P. rhoeas* date back to 1880, when the Reverend William Wilks, Vicar of Shirley, noticed a scarlet poppy with white edges on its petals growing in a cornfield next to his churchyard. He selected seed from this poppy and over a number of years managed to stabilise a reliably white-edged strain of poppies, as well as lilac, mauve and white forms, all of which became known as Shirley poppies. They are just as popular now as then, and there are singles as well as doubles with the charming pale hem.

P. commutatum from the Caucasus is another fine red annual poppy, and the gaudy colours of *P. nudicaule* the Iceland poppy have also been seen in European gardens for many years.

Poppy seed can be stored or left buried for many years to germinate eventually when soil is turned and the seed is exposed to light. This is why only herbicides eradicate them from cornfields where the ground is regularly turned. No one can forget images of the battlefields of Northern France where red corn poppies sprung up all over the ground disturbed by trenches and mass graves as the scars of the First World War began to settle. Annual papaver species like sun, while perennial species are content in dappled shade and the increasingly popular Himalayan poppies (*Meconopsis*) require much damper and shadier conditions.

Pelargonium

GERANIACEAE

pelargonium, bedding geranium, zonal geranium

Pelargoniums are often still referred to as geraniums although they were separated from that genus in the last century. One telling difference would be that pelargoniums are tender and geraniums are the hardy garden cranesbills. Native to the Cape of Good Hope, the first pelargonium arrived in Britain in 1632 and was probably one of the scented-leaved varieties, but the first pelargoniums were probably grown in France by nurseryman René Morin in Paris in 1621. The major influx of pelargoniums didn't occur until 1690, via Holland, and Britain was soon eager to encourage new species, particularly scented-leaved types varying in appearance from the 18 inch (45cm) plants of apple-scented *P. fragrans* and its cultivars to 3–4 feet (90–120cm) tall peppermint-scented *P. tomentosum* plants; some with smooth and some with heavily felted leaves. They were used very early on to flavour foods and drinks, to strew and use in potpourri.

After 50 years or so emphasis shifted away from obsession with scented foliage, particularly when *P. zonale*, with its thick truss of bright scarlet blossoms, arrived in Britain in the early 18th century. *P. zonale* effectively changed the way gardeners looked at pelargoniums but it was probably not one of the parents to father what became known as the zonal geraniums. These were more likely derived from *P. frutetorum* which had a mass of large dark salmon flower trusses held proudly above rounded leaves marked with black horseshoes, and slightly musky smelling. By modern standards, it was a straggly plant. *P. inquinans*, the scarlet geranium arrived in Britain shortly after *P. zonale*, also from the Cape of Good Hope and breeders rushed to develop improved strains. By the beginning of the 1800s, zonal geraniums were no longer straggly and had much broader flowers of rose, scarlet, magenta or salmon although white forms weren't developed until some time around 1850. The first double flowering hybrids came in 1864 and were available in salmon only, with a white double version following close on its heels. In the mid-1850s fancy-leaved geraniums also began appearing. The first was 'Attraction', a silver-variegated pelargonium no longer available. Then a gold-margined plant appeared followed by many variations.

There is a huge range of pelargoniums, from low bushy trailing types to shrubby plants several feet tall. Pelargoniums are generally grown in containers or summer tubs, best in fairly rich soil and kept slightly moist but never drowned. All cultivars should be propagated from cuttings and species from seed.

Petunia

SOLANACEAE

balcony petunia, climbing petunia

Perhaps petunias shouldn't really be called old-fashioned flowers as they haven't been with us very long, but the modern hybrids have been developed out of all recognition from the original species, so it is worth looking for old-fashioned petunias. In 1823, *Petunia axillaris*, the white petunia, arrived from its native South America, picked up by an explorer at the mouth of the Rio de la Plata. The deep magenta *P. integrifolia* (formerly *P. violacea*) arrived from Brazil soon afterwards.

This old-fashioned petunia produces a mass of small single trumpet-shaped flowers throughout the summer months and has a marked sweet scent, particularly apparent in evening. The plants have a slightly straggly sprawling habit and drop their heads down, best in pots and tubs where their blossoms fall enthusiastically over the edges. By 1880, there were double and grandiflora forms of the scented *P. integrifolia*. But the flowers were much less showy than those of modern hybrids. These can be found in almost every colour of the rainbow in singles, doubles and frilly pompoms; the heads don't nod so deeply as the old-fashioned varieties, stems are dwarfer and heads almost smother the foliage so they are considered suitable for extravagant bedding displays, but all lacking scent.

Fortunately, the fragrant *P. integrifolia* is coming back into fashion along with early hybrids, called balcony, climbing or pendula petunias, selected for the whites and purples that displayed the best fragrance.

The older varieties are just as easy to grow as their modern counterparts. For the best displays sow seed in autumn and overwinter in a cold frame before planting in spring. Don't plant petunias in very rich soil or they will produce foliage at the expense of flowers. They need regular watering to prevent them from wilting, and regular deadheading to ensure the longest flowering season.

Reseda

RESEDACEAE

mignonette

It is strange that mignonette seems to fallen completely out of fashion in gardens and is now rarely seen, despite the fact it is so easy to grow and produces very richly scented little flowers. Some say that the Romans brought it into Northern Europe from the southern Mediterranean before the 1st century and used the little herb as a sedative, dubbing it *resedare*, meaning to calm, but it only became popular in the 18th century when it was adopted by the French who called the plant *mignonette* or "little darling". Another story of its introduction suggests that seed was sent to the Empress Josephine from Egypt by Napoleon after his conquest of that country, so she could raise plants in her garden at Malmaison. Whatever the real origin, it was widely grown in southern France in the 18th and 19th centuries, and its flowers were used for making perfume.

Despite its rather dull pale flowers and sprawling habit mignonette became equally popular in England in the second half of the 18th century, and the strong fragrance rose from town windowboxes everywhere, particularly in London where it seemed to thrive despite pollution. Victorians later grew it widely in pots in cold conservatories and used it as a fragrant indoor decoration for parties.

R. odorata is a perennial plant in its warmer native countries where it has escaped from gardens and grows wild in abandoned ground. In Britain it is best to sow seed directly into a warm flower bed where they are to flower, although some people raise seedlings in a greenhouse for planting out in position.

Tagetes

COMPOSITAE

marigold

The French marigold, *Tagetes patula*, was discovered towards the end of the 16th century in the wilds of Mexico and Guatemala, and quickly adopted into Europe. French marigolds are bushy annuals growing up to 18 inches (45cm) with feathery scented leaves and daisy-like flowers. The earliest French marigolds were pale yellow, the range later being increased to include orange and reddish brown blossoms, single, double and quilled varieties.

Tagetes erecta, the African marigold, was found growing wild along the North African coast before it came into Britain at approximately the same time as the French marigold. Plants are much larger than French marigolds, growing up to 5 feet (150cm) tall with small 2–4 inch (5–10cm) flowers on top, varying from pale lemon to deep orange. Double African marigolds already existed by the mid-18th century, but they disappeared sometime afterwards, being reintroduced as a 20th century novelty.

The early French marigolds were rather small and not guaranteed to blossom well unless it was reliably hot and sunny; most of the development on these plants didn't occur until the end of the 19th century when reliable strains were bred, and it wasn't until the 1950s that popular modern dwarf French marigolds were created.

Curiously, many people considered the leaves of marigolds to smell offensive, particularly florists using them widely for bouquets, and a scentless variety was apparently first available in the mid-18th century to make the flower more pleasant for handheld bouquets. In 1937, David Burpee was proud to announce the first scentless marigold, 'Crown of Gold', and a race of non-scented hybrids followed. The edible-flowered *T. tenuifolia* or Signet marigold is preferable, with bright yellow single flowers, lacy foliage and lemon-scented leaves.

Marigolds are traditionally considered very useful companion plants, deterring aphids and other pests. However, modern scentless hybrids are of little use, dissuading few of the predators they originally deterred. The original tall African marigolds seem to have the strongest effect, so look for older forms if you want to use marigolds among your vegetables.

Marigolds are easy to please, tolerating most soils and conditions, from drought to soaking, but they do prefer a sunny location. Deadhead them frequently to encourage branching. Marigolds are propagated by seed which is easy to save but will not be very satisfactory from most new hybrids.

Tropaeolum majus

TROPAEOLACEAE

nasturtium, Indian cress

Nasturtiums come from the same family as watercress, and the common name is applied to two plants native to Colombia and Peru, the common nasturtium *Tropaeolum majus*, and *T. minus* which is now rare, although both were brought to Europe in the 15th century. Names often change through the ages and both species were once known as lesser or greater Indian cress, or *Nasturtium indicum*. Parkinson called nasturtiums yellow larkspur, others referred to them as yellow larksheele, although these common names were also applied to several completely different plants.

Gerard grew nasturtium for its flowers in his garden in 1597, identified as lesser Indian cress or *T. minus*. A century later various commentators identified greater Indian cress *T. majus* growing in several gardens but there seems to have been considerable confusion over names. Both types were certainly being recommended as salad herbs by the middle of the 17th century. But while *T. majus* outgrew the boundaries of vegetable beds and escaped into the flower garden fairly early on, *T. minus* stayed behind for medicinal and kitchen uses; it was on the National Council for the Conservation of Plants and Gardens (NCCPG) Pink Sheet (*see page 84*), but is fortunately available once again from a few nurseries. Double nasturtiums were introduced from Italy in 1769.

T. majus has brightly coloured, almost pansy-like blossoms on exuberant plants from early summer through till the first frosts and occurs naturally in shades of red, orange and yellow with a spur jutting from the rear of each blossom. They must have been a welcome addition to early cottage gardens. As well as their floral qualities, seeds can be used as a substitute for capers in pickles, leaves add a peppery taste to salads, and the flowers and buds were once also pickled.

Nasturtiums were first encouraged for their ability to clamber vigorously over fences, mounds and trellises; dwarf, free-blooming types more appropriate as bedding plants were not developed until the mid 19th century when varieties with spots, blotches, shading and bands of colour were developed. Dwarf forms also appeared from the 1850s onwards, a result of crossing *T. majus* with *T. minus*, producing the Tom Thumb strain which is still available. 'Empress of India', which has dark leaves and brilliant crimson flowers is still widely grown and dates from the same period.

Nasturtiums are trouble-free to raise: seed sets easily and they grow in sun and partial shade. Moreover, the poorer the soil the more likely they are to flourish, so they are ideal to brighten a dull spot where little else will thrive; if you sow them in rich soil they will make a mass of leaves but very few flowers. As the season progresses you may need to cut plants back as they grow so fast they can become straggly, and deadhead them regularly to encourage continuous flowering.

Zinnia

COMPOSITAE

zinnia, Brazilian marigold, medicine hat

Native to Mexico, the first zinnia to immigrate into Britain was *Zinnia peruviana* (formerly known as *Z. pauciflora* or *Z. lutea*) which came from Paris in 1753. It's an untidy plant, branching loosely to 3 feet (90cm) in height and topped by small, muddy yellow or burnished scarlet daisy like flowers. Much more exciting was *Z. elegans* which arrived from South America in 1796: it was also tall but the scarlet and crimson blossoms were larger, each topped by a Mexican hat-like disc surrounded by a skirt of ray petals. *Z. elegans* was the parent of today's popular hybrids.

The first doubles appeared in France in 1856, but the strain wasn't stable, causing some irritation when seed arrived in America in 1861 and two-thirds of it turned out to be single. However, zinnias came into their own in America, probably due to the sunny, warm climate.

Zinnias have gone up and down in height – by 1886, a 40 inch (1m) strain was available under the impressive name of *Z. elegans robusta grandiflora plenissima*, the Giant or Mammoth strain. On the other hand the Lilliputian strain produced plants from 3–10 inches (7–25cm) tall. The Tom Thumb type which appeared at the end of the 19th century was described as "the largest possible flower on the smallest possible plant".

Zinnias like any good deep soil in a sunny garden; seedlings are happy with a cold damp start but they need sun to flower well.

CLIMBERS

Clematis

RANUNCULACEAE

traveller's joy, old man's beard

The clematis family of climbers encompasses huge diversity: there are plants with flower sizes ranging from 1–10 inches (2–25cm) across; low growing forms as well as those that clamber for many yards; evergreen as well as herbaceous species and cultivars. Native to Europe, Lebanon, the Caucasus, Northern Iran and Afghanistan, as well as the chalky south-eastern regions of Britain, *Clematis vitalba* was the first clematis to come into cultivation. Originally thought to be a grape and called Viticella-Woodebinde by the Anglo-Saxons of the 11th century, it was also called traveller's joy, according to Gerard, because anyone on a long journey was grateful to rest in its shadow. Despite the fact that it was a rampant vine, *C. vitalba* was invited into cottage gardens but it is far too vigorous to invite into modern gardens unless you are fortunate to have a piece of woodland or large wild garden; its small white flowers are fragrant but not terribly exciting compared to other clematis. The common name of old man's beard applies to the hairy seed that overtakes the vine after blossoms have faded. *C. vitalba* is still important as the primary rootstock for grafting less rampant species, but a better old-fashioned garden species is *C. flammula*, also definitely grown in the 16th century. This vigorous species is not unlike a refined *C. vitalba*, and is covered in tiny white sweetly scented flowers from August to October, followed by silky seed heads.

C. viticella is the most decorative of the early garden clematis, a native of Southern Europe with nodding dusky-rose blossoms, cultivated in cottage gardens since the 16th century. Its common name, virgin's bower, was credited to Hugh Morgan, apothecary to Elizabeth I. *C. viticella* flowers late so is at its best growing through other plants to give a late performance. It was first hybridised through the accidental cross of *C. viticella* with *C. integrifolia*, a non-vining species. But large-flowered hybrids didn't appear until the 1850s, when several Chinese species arrived in Britain by way of Japan. *C. alpina* was an earlier introduction from Southern Europe, introduced in 1792. It is ideal for small gardens, flowering in April and May with small nodding blue flowers with a white central tuft. Some years it can flower again in midsummer.

The everlastingly popular clematis *C. montana* blooms just after most alpina varieties. It arrived from its native China and the Himalayas in the early 19th century, a prolific early blossomer with a subdued almondy scent, now available in pink forms as well as the orginal white. A very rewarding climber, it is embarrassingly vigorous if you plant it in the wrong place.

The first work on hybridising clematis was accomplished in 1855 by Isaac Anderson-Henry of Edinburgh. Using one of the newly introduced

Oriental clematis, *C. lanuginosa* (an introduction made by Robert Fortune and blessed with the largest blossoms of any species), Anderson-Henry created the white flowered 'Henryi', still popular. Then George Jackman, a nurseryman from Woking, used *C. lanuginosa* to create *C.* x *jackmanii* in 1858, with masses of 4–5 inch (10–12cm) wide, star-shaped, purple blossoms smothering the vine in spring and again in late summer – it remains popular. This introduction was the start of an outbreak of hybridising, producing cultivars that are still popular today, despite new numbers of clematis being introduced every year – old favourites include *C.* 'Marie Boisselet', *C.* 'Perle d'Azur' and the later *C.* 'Gravetye Beauty'.

Some gardeners find clematis difficult to grow, but if you follow a few basic principles you should have little trouble. Plant clematis in a generous hole laced with well-rotted manure and bonemeal to encourage strong root growth. Plant them deep because clematis are subject to a fungus disease called clematis wilt which makes plants wilt from the top and die; the fungus can't affect any part below ground, so deep-planted clematis have plenty of buds to regrow if the plant does succumb to disease and has to be cut hard back. Clematis require shaded roots but sunny stems, so it is a good idea to grow a low growing plant at the foot of the clematis to act as an umbrella; you can place a stone at the base of the plant but this can impede water flow which can be a problem as clematis do like to be well watered. Feed them every year with seaweed or an organic fertiliser. Pruning is often also a question: as a rule of thumb you can leave the early Montana types to fend for themselves, simply cutting back to shape when they become too vigorous. Large free-flowering clematis which flower early, before June, should be cut back straight after flowering to within a couple of buds away from the main branches. Those that flower later in the year should be cut back hard to within 6 inches (15cm) of the ground in February.

Recommended

C. alpina 'Francis Rivis': this early *alpina* hybrid has bright blue flowers which are larger than most other cultivars; it flowers in late spring and early summer and may repeat flower if cut back straight after flowering.

C. 'Perle d'Azur': a vigorous variety introduced in 1885; its pale blueish purple flowers blossom from June to August and look stunning growing through dark foliage plants.

C. texensis 'Gravetye Beauty': introduced to Britain by William Robinson at the beginning of the 20th century; it has bright red upward-looking bell-shaped flowers from July to September, and its scrambling habit means it looks superb growing on walls or over low shrubs.

Humulus lupulus

CANNABACEAE

common hop, European hop, bine

Humulus lupulus is native throughout northern temperate regions and was so valued that it was used by the peasants of Bohemia and Bavaria in the 9th century as legal tender to pay land debts. Anglo-Saxons called it *hoppen* after their word for climb.

In a matter of weeks, a hop vine can cover a small building, climbing from 15 to 40 feet (5–13m) in a season. According to Pliny, the Romans had an answer to controlling this energetic and potentially invasive plant – they ate the young shoots asparagus-style in spring, and hops were grown in medieval monastic gardens for food as well as for brewing and as a sedative, to encourage sleep and quell hysteria and to relieve pain. But it's the female version of hops with its cone-shaped flowers that has been grown for centuries, provoking the British Parliament to pass a law in 1528 forbidding the use of that "pernicious weed" in brewing. Although the law was rescinded in 1603, hops production wasn't widespread until the end of the 17th century. Hops were grown in many cottage gardens as decoration, camouflage and to help bread to rise as well as for brewing.

As the name suggests, hops like moist humus-rich soil but once planted don't feed them any more as they are quite capable of fending for themselves and too rich an environment willl encourage ever more rampant leaf growth without producing many flowers. They need sturdy support or can be very effective growing through established hedges and trees but don't plant hops where they can bully weaker plants.

Recommended

H. lupulus aureus: comparatively new, but many people consider it an easier garden plant than the traditional hop as it is slightly less rampant and the golden leaved foliage is attractive. Grow the golden form for ornament and use the original rampant species if you want to try it for food; young shoots are delicious.

Ipomoea

CONVOLVULACEAE

morning glory

Morning glories are native to tropical America, arriving in Britain in 1621 when John Goodyer received seed from correspondents abroad of *Convolvulus major*, later classified as *Ipomoea purpurea*. Seed came via Italy and the annual *Ipomoea tricolor / Convolvulus tricolor* arrived the same year from Spain (*see p 143*).

John Goodyer described the blossoms of morning glory as "redd darke crimson velvet", noting that the blooms tend to last only a day, folding towards evening. Native to Mexico, this vine has rounded leaves and prolific small blossoms. It is a very welcome late summer flowerer, blooming prolifically at the end of the season from late summer until hit by frost. This is the species responsible for many popular "heirloom" varieties in the US.

Morning glories have always been more popular in North America than northern Europe; there they self-seed in many areas to decorate yards, farms and roadsides without help. In Britain they have to be grown as annuals and have perhaps rarely been afforded the place they deserve, although they were a popular Victorian plant when bright coloured annuals really hit the headlines. However, the original morning glories were gorgeous only at dawn and closed shortly thereafter.

Meanwhile, while they were patently ignored in most parts of the world, morning glories enjoyed something of a craze in Japan in the 1830s. Using *I. nil*, hybridisers created a strain of scarcely twining, large-flowering, brightly coloured blossoms with double flowers and bands of colour. Called *I. x imperialis*, those morning glories were used to honour the emperor, with the equivalent of $18.00 sometimes spent on a single seed. Although there was little interest in that strain elsewhere, *I. nil* was introduced into the United States in 1895. It is responsible for many of the red-flowering hybrids, most notably 'Scarlett O'Hara'.

I. alba (formerly *Calonyction alba*), commonly called the moonflower, was popular in North America during the Victorian era when white evening gardens were in vogue. It has white blossoms creased in cream which have a jasmine-like scent, growing on vines that can reach 30 feet (10m) in long-season areas, but it dislikes cool evenings so never really caught on in Northern Europe.

In 1963, it was discovered that chewing the seeds could cause hallucinations. The sales of morning glories dropped off drastically in the United States and their purchase was prohibited briefly in Britain. Many varieties were lost to cultivation but morning glories seem to be enjoying something of a resurgence at present.

They need a sunny position in poor soil, ideally east facing, and they need a reasonable amount of water or they wilt. Strong support is necessary as the weight of a fully grown morning glory can topple something too slight, especially in high winds. Seed forms readily, but different varieties cross-pollinate freely so should not be grown together if you want to save seed. When germinating, nick and soak the seed; it sprouts rapidly, and either wait until May and sow direct into the ground or start seeds off earlier indoors. In fact there's little advantage in starting seeds early as they bloom late in the summer whatever your schedule.

Recommended

I. purpurea 'Grandpa Ott': Grandpa Ott's morning glory (*see page 96*) was responsible for the foundation of the Seed Savers Exchange in the USA where Kent and Diane Whealy work to preserve seeds of endangered plants. Grandpa Ott's produces a mass of deep purple blossoms accented by a yellow star in the throat. Seed was originally brought over from Bavaria in the 19th century by Baptist John Ott who grew the vine each summer.

Following his death, his granddaughter Diane Whealy realised the strain would be lost if she didn't continue to save the seed. That realisation led to the birth of the Seed Savers Exchange in 1975, branching into the Flower and Herb Exchange in 1990.

Dolichos lablab

LEGUMINOSAEA

hyacinth bean, Indian bean, Egyptian bean

The hyacinth bean is native to tropical Africa but widely in cultivation throughout India, Southeast Asia, Egypt and the Sudan. Grown as an annual, it was introduced from India in 1794. Although Europeans and Americans valued its large, flat, brick-red seed pods simply for their beauty, the hyacinth bean is an important food crop in its native region, eaten in the same manner as kidney beans. Not only are the bean pods handsome, but they are also preceded by purple blossoms against dark, deeply textured, segmented leaves.

Before the hyacinth bean was grown in 19th century cottage gardens, where it neatly straddled the gap between food and flower, it began its career under cultivation in the glasshouse. In Victorian times, the violet-coloured variety was known as 'Darkness', often planted against a white-flowering bean from Japan known as 'Daylight' which is still available. A vigorous vine, the hyacinth bean can climb to heights of 10 feet (3m) if given full sun. However, like most beans, don't give a lablab too much fertiliser as they do best on a lean diet. Moisture is essential as they dry out very rapidly. It's advisable to start seeds early, transplanting when the soil turns warm, and watch out for caterpillars and other legume eaters. Hyacinth beans make a handsome companion to support morning glories.

Jasminum

OLEACEAE

jasmine, jessamine, poet's jasmine

Native to Asia Minor, the Himalayas and China, the common white jasmine *Jasminum officinale* was growing in cottage gardens some time before 1577 when Thomas Hill recommended planting the vine to improve city air. He suggested combining the loose, leaning vine with roses, which is still a sound suggestion. Jasmine produces numerous small white very fragrant flowers; if you grow it near a window your house will be perfumed all summer long.

By 1629, John Parkinson wrote that *J. officinale* could be encountered "ordinarily in our gardens throughout the whole land", as popular in humble or great gardens, although it requires a sheltered position against a south wall to flourish in colder areas. In France jasmine has been grown commercially for hundreds of years for perfume.

Jasmines prefer reasonably rich soil but are quite happy to grow in partial shade, making very good companions for other climbers. They don't need much water but they can be rather short lived unless very well looked after. There will be dieback in a hard winter so it is essential to prune jasmine hard in spring when it is not blossoming to maintain a good shape and a healthy plant.

Lathyrus

LEGUMINOSEAE

perennial sweet pea

Although people are most familiar with the annual sweet pea *L. odoratus* (*see below*), surprisingly little space is given to their attractive ancestors. *L. sativus* is known to have been cultivated 8,000 years ago along eastern Mediterranean coasts and its sky blue cultivar *L. s.* var. *azureus* has been grown in England for over 200 years; there are also forms with all white or blue and white flowers.

Though not a British native, *L. latifolius* was a cottage garden favourite from early days, a vigorous climbing perennial producing numerous stems of 6 feet (180cm) or more each year, with up to 15 magenta-pink flowers on each stem. Some forms have pale pink and white flowers. The narrow-leaved everlasting pea, *L. sylvestris*, is a British native with slightly smaller greenish pink flowers. Among other good climbing perennials is *L. rotundifolius*, native to Central Asia, grown in Britain since the mid 19th century.

Recommended

L. nervosus: Lord Anson's blue pea was brought from Patagonia in 1744 and boasts clear blue perfumed flowers. Look for it, ask for it, and see if you can encourage nurseries to find and propagate it more widely.

L. rotundifolius: oval to round leaflets and brick red flowers blooming profusely in May and June. It climbs rapidly to 6 feet (180cm) and needs space.

L. tuberosus: the Fyfield pea, a lightly scented British native with rich rosy pink flowers, widely grown in the 18th century. Although smaller than *L. rotundifolius* it spreads under the ground and can be invasive in light soils.

L. cirrhosis: bright pink flowers blossom for most of the summer over blue-grey narrow leaves; this species scrambles to form a dense 2–3 feet (60–90cm) mound.

Lathyrus odoratus

FABACEAE

annual sweet pea

Native to Italy, Crete and Sicily, the annual *Lathyrus odoratus* was so potently fragrant that it caught the eye – and nose – of the Franciscan monk, Father Cupani. In 1696 he found the plant in Sicily, collected it and planted the seed in his monastery garden. The fragrance is extraordinary, resembling the mixed perfume of honey, propolis and wax that rushes from a freshly opened beehive. The monk sent seed in 1699 to a horticultural friend in Britain, Dr Robert Uvedale of Enfield. That same seed was made commercially available in 1724 and is again offered by specialist seedsmen under the name 'Cupani's Original', or 'Matucana'.

The original sweet pea remained untouched but very popular for the next century. Then, in the early 19th century, the colour range was increased until varieties were available in colours including pinks, blues, purples, white and combinations of those shades. All of those original sweet peas were fragrant, but the look of sweet peas altered in 1870 when Henry Eckford created the larger flowered Grandifloras; this innovation was followed by the Unwins, a group with slightly waved petals. In 1900 the gardener at Althorp, the estate of the Earl and Countess Spencer, discovered 'Lady Spencer', a rose pink mutation of Henry Eckford's 'Prima Donna' sporting very large flowers with wavier edges on longer stems. Unfortunately it had little scent.

The Spencers revolutionised sweet peas, rendering them the most popular annual flower by 1910 but unfortunately a flurry of new developments meant that the earlier highly scented forms all but disappeared from the market. Some of the original fragrant originals have only recently been rediscovered.

Sweet peas are easy to grow. They prefer cool temperatures and quickly slip out of bloom when the weather becomes warm in summer. So they are best sown indoors or as soon as the ground has thawed in spring, then planted into loose soil with good support for them to climb up. Since they are self-fertile, sweet peas will not interbreed readily with their neighbours but sweet pea seeds begin to lose viability rapidly if not sown every year.

Recommended

L. odoratus 'Painted Lady': known in 1737 and recently collected from an Australian family who had kept it in cultivation for many generations, as well as over 50 other old-fashioned sweet peas.

L. odoratus 'Prima Donna': one of Henry Eckford's pink flowering, wavy-edged sweet peas, grown in 1896.

L. odoratus 'Black Knight': a deep maroon highly scented variety dating from 1898.

Lonicera

CAPRIFOLIACEAE

honeysuckle, woodbine

Native to Europe, Asia Minor, the Caucasus and Western Asia, *Lonicera periclymenum* was a common fixture in cottage gardens from the start, valued for its rich scent and easy habit. The original common form is still the best of all; it has gloriously scented creamy white flowers in summer, dark pink or yellow on the outside and darkening with age to be followed by attractive bright red berries. It is one of the plants that conjures up an instant evocative image of the English garden in summer.

The family name, *Caprifoliaceae*, refers to the fact that honeysuckle vines are a favourite food of browsing goats. For human consumption, Dioscorides suggested honeysuckle for fatigue, shortness of breath and hiccups as well as diseases of the lungs and spleen. Flowers have been used as a laxative and for respiratory ailments and asthma. Still a favourite plant in Britain, common honeysuckle has become a nuisance in America, strangling trees and covering ground invasively. Its planting is generally frowned upon.

Honeysuckle adapts well to most environments, growing happily in sun or shade, perhaps most at home when twined around an old apple tree, a porch or front wall, wafting its scent through bedroom windows. It tolerates drought as well as torrential rain – although in my experience it is not particularly happy when used for target practice by young footballers!

Recommended

L. periclymenum 'Belgica': the early Dutch honeysuckle has very scented reddish purple flowers that fade to yellow.

Passiflora

PASSIFLORACEAE

passion flower

Native to tropical America, few people believed the first sketch of a passionflower drawn by an Augustine monk returning from the New World to Rome in the early 1600s. But papal scholars quickly jumped at the flower's symbolic potential and even used the strangely configured flowers to help South American missionaries tell the Passion story to potential converts. They interpreted the 10 petals and sepals as representing the 10 apostles at the crucifixion of Jesus. The filaments were the crown of thorns or halo, the five anthers were the wounds and the three stigmas symbolised the nails.

That early passion flower was probably *Passiflora incarnata*, later called the maypop in North America, native as far north as Virginia and prone to a long dormancy period. Although it was taken to Britain it didn't lend itself readily to cultivation and was followed in 1690 by *P. caerulea*, the passion flower we grow today, as popular now as it was in early cottage gardens, sufficiently energetic to reach flowering size quickly, and producing large numbers of attractive flowers.

At the end of the 19th century passion flowers gained the attention of hybridisers (along with most other genera). The best cultivar was the athletic, free-flowering and fragrant hybrid *P. alato* x *caerulea* with large flowers of alternating white and pink petals. New species have recently been introduced after a lull of almost a century, notably the red-flowering *P. vitifolia* and *P. coccinea* as well as many new hybrids.

Passifloras require light sunny warm sites, with plenty of room to send their energetic arms and legs roaming – several will climb 9 feet (3m) or more in a single season. They like a rich soil and should be fed with organic fertiliser throughout the growing season for the best blossoms. You can grow them in a container, but make sure it is large enough as they have large roots and it can be difficult to untangle all the tendrils without a lot of damage if you have to transplant them.

Recommended
P. caerulea: the most popular passion flower, grown in England for over 300 years. It produces a mass of 3–4 inch (7–10cm) white flowers overlaid by a thick halo of blue filaments.

BULBS

Anemone

RANUNCULACEAE

windflower, garland anemone, rose parsley

In the second half of the 16th century many colourful plants were introduced into European gardens from Constantinople, among the most important being tulips, crown imperials, hyacinths, anemones, narcissi and lilies. Many of these plants were native to Western Asia but had already been cultivated for centuries in the Ottoman Empire (Turkey).

According to a Greek legend, Anemos, the wind, sent anemones to the ground as the earliest harbingers of his spring arrival. The Romans collected anemones to ward off fevers, while Gerard and Culpeper both suggested bathing in infusions of the native European wood anemones or windflowers, *Anemone nemorosa*, to ward off or cure leprosy, as well as suggesting the plant for a number of other ailments. Tradition suggests that *A. coronaria* earned its name when the Greeks and Romans made garlands, or coronets of the flowers. *A. coronaria* is native to Southern Europe and the Mediterranean, and it gained religious significance during the Crusades when the Bishop of Pisa suggested that ships returning from the Holy Land fill their holds with sacred soil on their return voyage; this resulted in the "miraculous" appearance of cherry red anemones wherever that soil was spread, prompting the church to suspect divine intervention. *A. coronaria* was widely distributed in monastery gardens because of its sacred connotations and by the 16th century a double form was widespread. Its common name, rose parsley, aptly describes the many-petalled blossoms that crown ferny, deep green foliage.

There were numerous species of anemones growing in Britain by the 16th century, so many that Gerard decided he could only bear to plant a dozen favourites in his garden, turning away many others, and by the end of the 17th century, 300 different species and varieties of anemones were identified in cultivation.

Although *A. blanda*, a native of the eastern Mediteranean, only became a popular garden plant in the 20th century, it appears that Theophrastus was familiar with it in about 300BC. The Japanese anemone, *A. japonica* (now *A. hupehensis*), is a recent cottage garden plant, introduced to Britain in 1845 by Robert Fortune. By the 1880s, pure white Japanese anemones were available, first called 'Alba', then 'Honorine Jobert', and still available under that name.

Anemones prefer a loose, alkaline, well-drained soil. The blossoms do not las t long, especially in hot, dry weather. *A. coronaria* is not reliably hardy and some people prefer to treat it as a greenhouse forcing bulb rather than growing it in open ground. Otherwise anemones are among the easiest bulbs to grow and multiply rapidly. Propagate by division.

Recommended

The 'St Brigid' group: at the end of the 19th century double anemones became known as the 'St. Brigid' group, in honour of an Irish columnist who wrote a celebrated garden column under the pen name of St. Brigid. 'Mount Everest', a semi-double snow white with a red band, is similar to the earliest double *A. coronaria*.

Colchicum

LILIACEAE

autumn crocus, naked boys, naked ladies, meadow saffron

The name colchicum is derived from their native Colchis, the ancient name for an area on the eastern side of the Black Sea. Colchicums extend from North Africa through Europe and Asia as far as the Himalayas. The leaves and corms of the plant contain a substance called colchicine which is poisonous to humans and animals; it was once recommended by the Arabians for the treatment of gout and in 18th century Europe it was much valued for this complaint. Today plant cytologists use it in plant breeding programmes to try and increase the number of chromosomes in plants.

Commonly known as autumn crocus or meadow saffron, both names are misleading as they are not crocuses and do not produce saffron. The common names naked boys or naked ladies are applied to most autumn-flowering colchicums. Their clusters of flowers emerge straight from the soil naked, without leaves, a striking sight as they open in glowing shades of pinks, purples and white. Leaves come after the flowers. Some colchicums flower in spring, these are largely tender species and best grown in an alpine house or tunnel.

Some fine colchicum species and hybrids have been recorded for centuries in Northern Europe. *C. autumnale* was introduced in 1753 and is still widespread and the soft lilac pink *C. byzantium* (*C. autumnale major*), praised by Clusius in 1601, is still a popular hybrid.

Most colchicums prefer to be planted in full sun but *C. autumnale* thrives on the edge of shrubberies or woodland. They appreciate light soil as long as it never dries out as they prefer a slightly damp environment.

Recommended

C. autumnale alboplenum: a good double white form, cultivated in Northern European gardens since the late 19th century.

C. variegatum: grown in northern Europe since 1753, is a very beautiful species with heavily chequered violet-pinkish flowers and small leaves.

C. alpinum 'De Candolle': a tiny species which came to Britain from alpine French and Swiss meadows at the beginning of the 19th century. It bears purplish pink solitary flowers.

Crocus

IRIDACEAE

crocus

The autumn-blooming saffron crocus, *Crocus sativus*, was grown in Palestine during Solomon's time and used in commerce in ancient civilisations as well as modern. Saffron comes from the Arabic *sahafarn*, which translates as "thread", referring to the stigmas that have proved so valuable economically. *Crocus sativus* was probably brought to Britain by the Romans; it was cultivated commercially in England by 1330, providing a yellow dye for fabrics and also a substitute for gold leaf in lettering. Saffron is one of the plants sometimes cited as an indicator of global climate change. Although it is easy to grow it does not flower easily in Northern Europe, needing a warmer climate. However, one small scale commercial grower is now growing saffron in Wales, so perhaps our climate is getting warmer again! Today saffron is usually imported from Turkey and Southern Europe to be used as a flavouring agent and to colour food.

The popular spring flowering ornamental *Crocus vernus* was also an early arrival, introduced to Europe from Constantinople by Clusius at the end of the 16th century. This crocus was among the bulbs credited with founding Holland's bulb industry along with tulips and hyacinths, crown imperials, narcissi and lilies. By the 1600s there were white, purple and striped forms. Other ornamental crocus family members also came from the Near East; the bright yellow *C. chrysanthus* was introduced in the 19th century and was much used for hybridising with *C. biflorus* to expand the colour range of spring crocus. Much of the breeding work was carried out by the famous 19th century English gardener E. A. Bowles in collaboration with Zwanenburg Nurseries in Holland, and some of their fine hybrids are still available today.

Crocus thrive in sunny positions in a light but fertile and well-drained alkaline soil. They perform best when they are taken up and divided every third year.

Recommended

C. chrysanthus 'Zwanenburg Bronze': created by E. A. Bowles at the end of the 19th century for the Zwanenburg nurseries; deep orange petals are heavily overlaid with purplish brown on the outside.

C. chrysanthus 'Snow Bunting': another E. A. Bowles cultivar, created at the beginning of the 20th century, white and cream flowers have prominent dark lilac feathering.

Cyclamen hederifolium

PRIMULACEAE

cyclamen, ivy-leafed cyclamen

Cyclamen are native to Southern Europe, Asia Minor and North Africa. Although many species are tender and common only as indoor plants, *Cyclamen hederifolium* is a delightful plant which never fails to produce pink flowers over leaves mottled with grey and white. It grows wild in Greece, Turkey and Italy.

The word cyclamen comes from the Greek *cyclos* meaning a circle, referring to the way the flower stem elongates after fertilisation, then coils to take the developing seed pod down to the ground. These plants were probably introduced to Northern Europe from Southern Italy in the 1500s, an alternative name has long been *C. neapolitanum*.

When flowers had to have a practical use before being invited into the garden, the roots were distilled and used as a remedy for toothache, earache and migraine. Gerard warned that pregnant women should avoid walking over the little flowers or else they might miscarry. Cyclamen seem to have been grown widely from the 17th century onwards, are completely hardy and very reliable, thriving best under trees in partial shade. *C. coum* is a very similar species, but introduced more recently.

Dry corms rarely germinate successfully but you can propagate cyclamen from seed collected as soon as it is ripe and sown immediately, no more than 1 inch (2.5cm) deep in moist fertile soil. The plants will self-seed and spread vigorously once established; clumps should be divided in autumn.

Dahlia

COMPOSITAE

dahlia

In 1575 travellers to Mexico found the native dahlia was already being cultivated, and doubles already existed so dahlias had probably been grown and selected by the Aztecs long before that date. But the first dahlias were not brought to Europe until 1798 when the Swedish botanist Andreas Dahl sent tubers of *Dahlia pinnata* and *Dahlia coccinea* to the Madrid Botanic Gardens, hoping they might be good to eat like potatoes. They never caught on. However, the large flowers of many colours were instantly popular in Europe.

By 1806, 55 single and semi-double cultivars were in flower at the Berlin Botanic Gardens and by 1808, the proto-typical double pom-pom type was bred by a Belgian breeder Monsieur Donckelaar, followed in 1809 by the first single white and in 1814 by large-flowering doubles. By 1818, the colour range had increased to include the full complement of rainbow shades now available. M. Donckelaar introduced dwarf dahlias in 1838.

During the 1830s dahlias became enormously popular in Britain and in 1841, one British dealer stocked over 1,200 varieties. At the turn of the century, 3,000 different dahlias were on the market. The flowers fell out of favour for the first two decades of the 20th century, but by the end of the 1920s they were popular again. Thousands of dahlias (with wonderful names such as 'Acme of Perfection', 'Dauntless' and 'Prince of Lilliputians') were available in the 19th century, but the majority of the older varieties have disappeared, although some can still be seen at the National Collection in Britain, among the collection holder's 2,000 cultivars and species.

Plant dahlias in very rich moist soil in full sun; the more humus and organic matter you put into the soil before planting, the better the size and colour of your blossoms. Keep their tuberous roots moist and well mulched throughout summer to ensure continuous blooms. All are tender except in the warmer parts of Britain, so you must lift them and store them over the winter to replant in spring. To harvest the tubers, wait until after the first light frost, then dig them up carefully, lay them in an airy place to dry then store them at a temperature of 4–10°C (40–50°F). If they get too hot or too cold they will rot or shrivel up.

Recommended

'Bishop of Llandaff': first produced in 1927, this cultivar is readily available; dark burgundy foliage is accented by plentiful single, scarlet flowers.

Erythronium dens-canis

LILIACEAE

dog's tooth violet

Erythronium dens-canis has been recorded in British gardens since 1596, and is native to deciduous woodland through much of Europe and Asia. The name refers to the bulb shape, which resembles a dog's tooth. The plant has bright green leaves mottled with darker green and brown, hence its common American name of toad lily. The flowers are white, pink or lilac with reflex petals that turn away from the purple anthers.

Plant slightly damp bulbs about 4 inches (10cm) deep in autumn in fertile well-drained but moist soil in partial shade. The easiest way to propagate is by dividing clumps straight after they have flowered in late spring.

Fritillaria

LILIACEAE

crown imperial, snakeshead fritillary

The first fritillary to reach Europe from its native southeast Turkey was the flamboyant crown imperial *Fritillaria imperialis*, introduced to Europe by Ogier Ghiselin de Busbecq, ambassador from the Holy Roman Emperor to Suleiman the Magnificent, at the Byzantine court. He saw it growing in the gardens of Suleiman the Magnificent and sent it with other bulbs (including tulips, hyacinths and anemones) in the diplomatic bag he sent back to Clusius at the court of Ferdinand I in 1560. It has a large naked bulb from which a stout stem rises to 3 feet (1m) with tiers of leaves which give off a foxy smell when bruised; pendulous cup-shaped flowers develop at the top of the stem.

In 1611, John Tradescant relates purchasing "fortye fritellarias at three pence a peece" from Holland. By the middle of the 18th century there was a vast choice in cultivation. The earliest kinds were orange, resembling medieval gold crowns, hence the name of *Corona imperialis* which was anglicised to crown imperial. They were also sometimes classified as *Lilium byzantium*.

Gerard grew many single orange crown imperials in his garden at Holborn in 1596, as well as what he termed a rare double. Parkinson liked the plant so much he gave it first place in his book *Paradisus in Sole*, 1629, and deep red and pale reddish yellow versions were recorded at the end of the 17th century. Interest in the plants waned for a while at the end of the 18th century before a renewed interest in exotic bulbs brought them back into fashion during the second half of the 19th century.

Other fritillaries were also brought to Europe in the 16th and early 17th centuries. The snakeshead fritillary *F. meleagris* was also growing in Gerard's garden, identified as the chequered daffodil or ginny-hen flower. Although it may have been introduced from the Balkans and western Russia, this species is also native to parts of southern England.

Crown imperials and snakeshead fritillaries flower well and increase if left undisturbed, but it is still a good idea to lift the bulbs occasionally, divide them and replant straight away in soil refreshed with compost and grit. Never let them dry out, and when you first try to establish a colony try and get hold of plants rather than dry bulbs which can be difficult and very slow to establish. If overcrowded you may end up with a number of non-flowering (blind) bulbs.

Galanthus

AMARYLLIDACEAE

snowdrop

Galanthus comes from the Greek *gala* for milk and *anthos*, flower, while the common name snowdrop originated from the 16th century *Schneetropfen* or snow pendant, reflecting the way the white heads hang down over the stems. The common snowdrop has been grown since earliest medieval times, but it is difficult to know what they were called in the past. Old herbals list them as *Leucoium bulbosum album*, meaning bulbous white violet.

The common snowdrop *G. nivalis* has been found in single and double (*flore pleno*) forms throughout Europe for centuries, but the great enthusiasm for snowdrops really took off in the 1850s when soldiers returned from the Crimean War with *G. plicatus* in their packs. It flowered later and was taller than the common snowdrop, growing well in shade and hybridising easily with other species. One of the earliest named hybrids, 'Straffan', was brought back from the Crimea by Lord Clarina and named after his home in southern Ireland, It is a clearer white than many cultivars, with distinctive green markings inside the flower, and plants usually produce two flowers per bulb so prolonging the flowering season.

Snowdrops were eagerly sought by Victorian plant hunters, and avidly collected by British gardeners. In the 1870s *G. elwesii* arrived from Turkey, shortly followed by the slightly tender *G. fosteri*, native from southern Turkey to as far south as the Lebanon. One of the mainstays of most snowdrop collections today, the cultivar *G. nivalis* 'Atkinsii' was created at the end of the 19th century, named after a gardener at Painswick House in Gloucestershire, gardens which still display arguably the best snowdrop collection in Europe (*see page 183*).

Some of the late 19th century snowdrops are scented, such as the sweet smelling 'S. Arnott', a good clump forming cultivar that smells of honey and produces shining white drop-like flowers, but some people have compared the smell of 'William Thomson' to air freshener!

Snowdrops flourish in woodland conditions and prefer slightly alkaline soil. Don't enrich the soil with manure after planting but incorporate some garden compost into the soil when planting. Some growers recommend adding good quality beech leaf mulch annually. Snowdrops are easy to propagate; simply divide clumps after flowering and replant before the leaves die back. It is a good idea to divide the less strongly growing cultivars and species every two years while more robust snowdrops can be left for three or four years.

Recommended

G. elwesii: a very reliable but rather variable species. Leaves range from very narrow to as wide as an inch (2.5cm), and flowers vary in their inner markings but usually have a green arch around the notch of the inner segments and a separate marking at the base.

G. nivalis 'Atkinsii': one of the earliest snowdrops to appear; it has long flat leaves and long outer petals with an arrow shaped pale green mark on the inner segments. The flowerhead is initially shorter than the leaves but the plant grows taller as it flowers until the head crowns the leaves.

Hyacinthus

LILIACEAE
hyacinth, bluebell, scilla

Native to Turkey, Syria and Lebanon, the intensely fragrant *Hyacinthus orientalis* was traditionally worn in headdresses by bridesmaids in ancient Greek weddings. Hyacinths were introduced to Europe by Ghiselin de Busbecq (*see Fritillaria page 170*), sent in the package of bulbs from Constantinople to the botanist Clusius in Vienna in 1560. In 1592 Clusius took this bulb collection into the Low Countries when he went to run the Botanic Garden at Leiden, and this was the beginning of the Dutch bulb industry.

Hyacinths were popular very early on, with double white, blue and pink varieties available as early as 1613, and 2,000 different hyacinths in cultivation by 1730. The early doubles were rather different from the modern upright versions, with each flower on the spike drooping downward, and work on the development of the early hyacinths into our modern forms only began in the late 18th century. During the 19th century increasing numbers of hyacinths were produced for forcing indoors in hourglass-shaped vases of water, and many strong colours became available then, from dark blues to deep yellows.

Few of the early forcing hyacinths are available now; of the 84 different plants offered in an 1897 catalogue, only two are still available – 'Marie' an indigo-purple single introduced in 1860, and 'King of the Blues', a deep purple single introduced in 1863.

The attractive Roman hyacinth, *H. o. albulus* is native to southern France but was grown in Britain from the 17th century; it produces several small stems from each bulb, topped with loose white nodding flowerheads, rather similar to the original wild species. However, it is no longer commercially available.

Hyacinths are hardy and will grow successfully outside but they are most used for forcing indoors to flower from Christmas onwards. In the garden they prefer to be planted in a sunny warm spot in well-drained soil.

The English bluebell, Hyacinthoides non-scripta, with its smaller spires of packed blue bell-shaped blossoms, has been gracing patches of woodland and shady wasteland throughout Northern Europe for thousands of years. Easy to grow in any reasonably fertile soil, bluebells are excellent garden plants for wild gardens and to bring colour to borders in spring. White and pink forms are available as well as the familiar lilac-blue, but if you plant bluebells near an ants' nest, the formic acid will turn all blue blossoms pink. They will also produce pink blossoms when grown in very acid soil.

Narcissus

AMARYLLIDACEAE

narcissus, daffodil

There are native daffodil species to almost every area of Europe, as well as Northern Africa, Western Asia, China and Japan; the first daffodils grown in European gardens were probably *Narcissus tazetta*, known as the bunch-flowering narcissus or polyanthus narcissus. This yellow and orange multi-headed scented daffodil was grown by the ancient Greeks, and although it is not one hundred per cent hardy throughout Northern Europe, it is widely naturalised wherever climate suits. The oldest form is 'Grand Soleil D'Or', which might well coincide with Parkinson's *Narcissus africanus aureus major*, the yellow daffodil of Africa. By the 1880s *N. tazetta* var. *orientalis*, the Chinese sacred lily or Lien Chu lily, was very popular, billed by Victorian catalogues as producing no fewer than 97 flowers from a single bulb.

It is often assumed that the Latin name, narcissus, is connected with the youth who was so obsessed with his own image that he drowned while trying to embrace his image in a river, but Pliny insists that the name comes from *narkao*, to benumb, alluding to the bulb's narcotic qualities. Juice from the bulb, applied to an open wound, was said to cause instant numbness of the nervous system and paralysis of the heart.

N. poeticus, the fragrant poet's narcissus, was mentioned by Theophrastus in 320BC. Usually considered a native of France and Switzerland, it is widely naturalised throughout southern Europe. Daffodils have been firmly established in European gardens for 300 years or more, with doubles particularly popular in the 17th century. The first garden daffodils tended to have nodding heads, relatively small flowers and spindly flower stems compared to their modern counterparts but hybridisation began seriously in the 1820s and the resulting plants were often stronger with larger flowers. Between 1860 and 1900 one thousand new daffodils were introduced with a further 6,000 appearing by 1930.

Daffodils are ideal candidates for naturalising, tolerating most soils and light conditions, from full sun to semi-shade. The only prerequisite is well-drained soil, which should ideally not be too light. Plant bulbs 4-6 inches (10–15cm) deep in autumn, and divide after a few years when clumps begin to get established, as they always flower best if they aren't too crowded.

Recommended

N. pseudonarcissus syn. *N. lobularis*: the Lent lily or wild daffodil has been growing wild in Northern Europe for centuries. It is an ancient and therefore rather variable daffodil with very erect leaves and small yellow trumpets with small paler yellow or cream petals surrounding them.

N. poeticus 'Plenus': dates from the 18th century. It produces single strongly fragrant double snowy white open faced flowers with tiny red-tipped cups.

N. poeticus var. *recurvus*: known in Britain from the early 1700s. Sometimes called 'Old Pheasant's Eye', its flowers also have red-tipped cups but glistening white curved back petals.

Lilium

LILIACEAE

lily

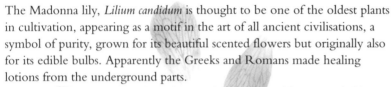

The Madonna lily, *Lilium candidum* is thought to be one of the oldest plants in cultivation, appearing as a motif in the art of all ancient civilisations, a symbol of purity, grown for its beautiful scented flowers but originally also for its edible bulbs. Apparently the Greeks and Romans made healing lotions from the underground parts.

Native from Greece to the Lebanon, the Madonna lily was probably brought to Northern Europe by the Romans, it was definitely growing at Walafrid Strabo's garden at Reichenau in the 10th century. Its broad, unwavering white trumpets produce a wonderfully rich perfume from their numerous 3–4 inch (7–10cm) wide waxy white flowers. In order to blossom, Madonna lilies require about three months of sunshine and their bulbs should never be covered with more than about an inch (2.5cm) of soil. They can be slightly fussy to establish, unlike another old favourite, the Turk's cap lily, *L. martagon*. Native to southeastern Europe but grown in northern Europe since at least 1596, the martagon lily has about 20 pink flowers per stem with petals that curve back to form a turban shape. They naturalise well and some people use them in informal wild garden plantings. Lilies and martagons were widely grown but still seen as separate species when Parkinson wrote *Paradisi in Sole, Paradisus Terrestris* in 1629.

L. chalcedonicum is another lily from Greece, widely grown in northern Europe by the 18th century, with bright red hanging flowers which gave it its common name of fiery lily. By the 19th century tiger lilies *L. lancifolium* had been introduced into Northern Europe from Asia, their backward curving black spotted orange flowers soon becoming firm favourites in cottage gardens and grander borders alike. In 1862 the impressive late summer flowering golden-rayed lily *L. auratum* was introduced from Japan. Displaying very fragrant ivory flowers spotted in purple with a central band of yellow, this has never been easy to grow in Britain, requiring a rather warmer climate, but is an ideal plant for the conservatory.

The regal lily *L. regale*, introduced from China at the end of the 19th century by the great plant hunter E. H. Wilson, is one of the best white garden lilies, easier to grow than the Madonna lily. Regal lilies grow to six feet (2m) tall with up to 20 fragrant trumpets which are white on the inside and pinkish purple on the outside.

The most important thing to remember when cultivating lilies is that they must have good drainage in deep rich soil, so you will need to add grit to heavy soil when you plant bulbs 4–6 inches (10–15cm) deep. If lilies sit in wet ground they will fail. Most lilies prefer to have their roots in shade but their heads in the sun, and many thrive in dappled shade or on the edge of woodland areas. Tall varieties will need to be staked unless there are other plants to support them. The Madonna lily has slightly different cultivation requirements preferring to be planted in a sunny spot in autumn with no more than 1½ inches (4cm) of soil over the bulb. As with other bulbs, when plants begin to go straggly and produce less blossoms, divide them. New divisions may not bloom for two or three seasons after transplanting.

Recommended

L. pyrenaicum: the Pyrenean lily has been cultivated in Britain since the 16th century; it produces spikes with at least ten small greenish yellow spotted and lined Turk's cap flowers, on 3-4 foot (90–120cm) tall plants.

L. x testaceum: one of the oldest hybrids in cultivation, developed from *L. chalcedonicum* and *L. candidum* in the 1830s. Groups of flowers appear at the top of 4 foot (120cm) stems, fragrant creamy yellow petals curving back to display bright orange anthers. Cultivation requirements are similar to those of the Madonna lily: full sun in very well-drained soil.

Tulipa

LILIACEAE

tulip

In the second half of the 16th century many colourful plants were introduced into European gardens from the Ottoman Empire (Turkey), among the most important being tulips, crown imperials, hyacinths, anemones, narcissi and lilies. Many of these plants were native to Western Asia but had already been cultivated for centuries in Constantinople.

Ogier Ghiselin de Busbecq (*see Fritillaria page 170*) first came across tulips in 1555, seeing them for the first time during a winter trip between Adrianople and Constantinople. He paid a considerable amount for bulbs and seeds and sent them to the great botanist Clusius at the imperial court in Vienna. In 1578, tulips arrived in Britain, and when Gerard wrote in 1597, seven types were available including a red, a yellow and a streaked sort.

In 1592 Clusius took his tulip collection into the Low Countries when he went to the Botanic Garden at Leiden. Apparently, many of those original bulbs were stolen, and tulip bulbs became incredibly sought after. It was soon noticed that some tulips would split to produce a flower that was feathered or flamed with stripes and splashes of another colour, and these became known as Rembrandt tulips as they were popular subjects for painters. Since 1928 we have known that that this was due to a virus spread by aphids, but at the time it led to an outbreak of buying and selling bulbs as commodities for huge inflated prices – "tulipomania". Tulips were briefly an important trading commodity.and at the peak of tulipomania in 1634 fortunes were gained and lost over tulip speculation, with bulbs sold for magnificent sums to people who knew nothing about horticulture, but the market collapsed soon after, with speculators and bulb merchants falling into debt. The virus generally weakened the Rembrandts, as flamed tulips were called, and few tulips survive from that time. However, Hortus Bulborum, the Dutch national bulb museum, has recently made some excess bulbs available so that 'Lack Van Rijn', a red pointed-petalled tulip with white edging (from 1620) and 'Zomerschoon' with ivory petals flamed in red (also dating from 1620) are now available.

Trends in tulips changed with time. Frilly edged parrot tulips date back to the 1600s. Most cottage gardeners from the 17th century on also grew the short-stemmed 'Duc Van Thol' types, which slipped from fashion in the early 20th century and are rare at present. Darwin tulips, developed from antique Flemish varieties, were all the rage in the late 19th century, 'Clara Butt' (pink flowering, circa 1889) was the most popular and is still available. Of the parrot tulips, 'Fantasy' (pink, with apple-green markings, *c.*1910) is the oldest still to be found.

Plant tulips in late autumn, sinking the bulbs 4–6 inches (10–15cm) into sandy soil enriched with loam and leaf mould. Tulips dislike soggy soil and prefer to be baked in the sun in order to thrive and produce new bulbs. If swamped with the foliage of surrounding plants you may need to replace bulbs every few years. Otherwise propagate by dividing bulbs every three years once groups are established.

Recommended

T. 'Pink Beauty': this single early flowering cultivar, raised by Barrs and Dibbats in 1889, has deep pink petals edged with white.

T. 'La tulipe noire': the petals of this 19th century Darwin tulip are predominantly deep purple, sometimes suffused with a touch of dark pink.

T. 'Keizerskroon': raised before 1750, the inner petals of this very attractive single early cultivar are pinkish red fringed with yellow, and the outer petals are pinkish red bordered with creamy white.

THE DIRECTORY — RESOURCES

ORGANISATIONS

National Council for the Conservation of Plants and Gardens (NCCPG)

For membership enquiries contact:
The Pines
Wisley Garden
Woking
Surrey GU23 6QP
Tel: 01483 211465
Fax: 01483 211750

The *Directory of National Plant Collections* is published annually by the National Council for the Conservation of Plants and Gardens.
Members receive *Plant Heritage*, a journal with information on many nurseries and open gardens.
See page 84.

Royal Horticultural Society

80 Vincent Square
London SW1P 2PE
For membership enquiries:
Tel: 0171 821 3000
Fax: 0171 828 2304
web: http://www.rhs.org.uk/

Britain's prime horticultural charity which promotes good gardening practice. It has experimental and show gardens, principally at Wisley in Surrey, organises the annual Chelsea Flower Show and many smaller shows, runs numerous gardening courses and produces *The Garden* magazine monthly. The RHS publishes *The Plant Finder* annually, listing all species, cultivars and varieties known to be grown by nurseries in the UK. The RHS also publish many excellent guides and booklets on aspects of gardening. Members receive *The Garden* plus free entry to many gardens of particular interest throughout the UK.

Henry Doubleday Research Association

Ryton Organic Gardens
Coventry CV8 3LG
Tel: 01203 303517
Fax: 01203 639229
email: enquiry@hdra.org.uk

The HDRA is the champion of organic gardening in the UK and Europe's main campaigning organisation to preserve diversity. It runs a Heritage Seed Library for members, sponsors international research and has many local groups. HDRA members receive a quarterly magazine and discount from the mail order seed and plant catalogue, plus free entry to the HDRA's demonstration gardens, at Ryton near Coventry and Yalding in Kent.

Hardy Plant Society

Mrs Pam Adams
Little Orchard
Great Comberton
Pershore
Worcestershire WR10 3DP
Tel: 01386 710317

Charity which encourages the growing of hardy plants, especially herbaceous perennial plants. It organises plant sales, runs a Members' Open Garden scheme and a seed exchange for members who also receive *The Hardy Plant* journal quarterly.

Cottage Garden Society

c/o Clive Lane
'Brandon'
Ravenshall,
Betley, Cheshire CW3 9BH
Tel: 01270 820258 (evenings)
Fax: 01270 250118

Formed in 1982, the Society aims to keep alive the tradition of gardening in the cottage style. Members receive a quarterly newsletter, the opportunity to take part in an annual seed distribution scheme, and the chance to visit members' open gardens.
See page 52.

Plantlife

The Natural History Museum
Cromwell Road
London SW7 5BD
Tel: 0171 938 9111

Plantlife is Britain's wild plant conservation charity, working to conserve wild plants in their natural habitats. It manages habitats and nature reserves and is actively involved in revitalising wild populations of endangered plant species. Members receive *Plantlife* magazine quarterly, plus a programme of events throughout the country.

SPECIALIST NURSERIES

There are hundreds of marvellous specialist nurseries; the following list does not attempt to be comprehensive but we hope the selection provides a good starting point.

As the cost of catalogues can change, we haven't included this information in the entries. Please, don't expect catalogues for nothing, but contact the nursery and send the appropriate money or stamped addressed envelope.

Apple Court
Hordle Lane
Hordle
Lymington
Hampshire SO41 0HU
Tel: 01590 642130
Fax: 01590 644220

Hostas, daylilies, grasses, ferns, unusual perennials and foliage plants.

Avon Bulbs
Burnt House Farm
Mid-Lambrook
South Petherton
Somerset TA13 5HE
Tel: 01460 242177

The widest selection of bulbs in the United Kingdom.

David Austen Roses
Bowling Green Lane
Albrighton
Wolverhampton WV7 3HB
Tel: 01902 376300
Fax: 01902 372142
Orders: 01902 376377

Specialist grower of shrub and old-fashioned roses, hybrid tea and floribunda roses, and breeder of 'English Roses'. Also an interesting selection of perennial garden plants, daylilies, irises and paeonies.

Steven Bailey Nursery
Sway
Lymington
Hampshire SO41 6ZA
Tel: 01590 682227
Fax: 01590 683765

Alstroemeria specialist.

Peter Beales Roses
London Road
Attleborough
Norfolk NR17 1AY
Tel: 01953 454707
Fax: 01953 456845
email: sales@classicroses.co.uk
web: www.classicroses.co.uk

Old-fashioned and classic rose specialist, with a good selection of hybrid tea roses as well. Thousands of container-grown roses, for collection only, and some 250 classic roses unique to the nursery. Very comprehensive, beautifully illustrated catalogue.

Beth Chatto Gardens
Elmstead Market
Colchester
Essex CO7 7DB

Wide selection of herbaceous plants.

Bernwode Plants
Kingswood Lane
Ludgershall
Aylesbury
Bucks HP18 9RB
Tel: 01844 237415
Fax: 01844 238920
email: email@bernwodeplants.co.uk

Specialising in growing historic plants, including many cottage garden perennials. *See page 72.*

The Botanic Nursery
Atworth, Melksham
Wiltshire SN12 8HY
Tel: 0850 328756 mobile
Fax: 01225 700953

Holding a National Collection of foxgloves, the nursery specialises in European species and primary forms of *Digitalis purpurea* as well as other perennial plants.

Ann and Roger Bowden
Sticklepath
Okehampton
Devon EX20 2NL
Tel: 01837 840481
Fax: 01837 840482

Wide range of hostas from National Collection holder.

Bridgmere Nurseries
Bridgemere
near Nantwich
Cheshire CW5 7QB
Tel: 01270 521100
Fax: 01270 520215

The nurseries offer a wide range of perennial plants and hold the National Collection of *Clematis orientalis*. No mail order.

Broadleigh Gardens
Bishops Hull
Taunton
Somerset TA4 1AE
Tel: 01823 286231

Specialist small bulb grower and holder of National Colelction of narcissus.

Catforth Gardens Nursery
Catforth Gardens
Roots Lane, Catforth
Preston PR4 0JB
Tel: 01772 690561

A wide range of geraniums offered by a National Collection holder.

Chipchase Castle Nursery
Wark
Hexham
Northumberland
Tel: 01434 230083

Cottage garden and herbaceous plants, many historic species and cultivars.

Crowther Nurseries
Ongar Road
Abridge
Essex RM4 1AA
Tel: 01708 688581
Fax: 01708 688677

A wide range of clematis offered by a National Collection holder.

D'Arcy & Everest
St Ives Road
Somersham, Huntingdon
Cambridgeshire PE17 3ET
Tel: 01487 843650
Fax: 01487 840096

Rare and unusual plants; alpines from around the world.

Derek Lloyd Dean
8 Lynwood Close
South Harrow
Middlesex HA2 9PR

The specialist grower and holder of the National Collection of angel pelargoniums offers a wide range of pelargoniums by mail order.

Carl Denton
The Cottage
Adel Willows
Otley Road
Leeds LS16 8AF
Tel: 0113 2612205
email: Trilliums@compuserv.com

Specialist trillium grower and holder of the National Collection offers widest possible range – along with mountains of helpful advice.

Fibrex Nurseries
Honeybourne Road
Pebworth
Nr Stratford upon Avon
Warwickshire CV37 8XT
Tel: 01789 720788
Fax: 01789 721162

Wide range of herbaceous plants offered by the holders of a National Collection of pelargoniums – they hold 200+ species and several thousand cultivars.

Foxgrove Plants
Foxgrove Farm, Enborne
Newbury RG14 6RE
Tel: 01635 40554

Smaller decorative, chiefly herbaceous plants, especially primulas, saxifrages and violas, as well as an exceptional range of snowdrops.

Peter Grayson
Sweet Pea Seedsman
34 Glenthorne Close
Bramton, Chesterfield
Derbyshire SY0 3AR
Tel: 01246 278503

Excellent range of sweet peas including many historic varieties.

Hardy's Cottage Garden Plants
Freefolk Priors
Freefolk, Whitchurch
Hampshire RG28 7NJ
Tel: 01256 896533
Fax: 01256 896572

Wide range of herbaceous perennials, old favourites and less common plants.

Hexham Herbs
Chesters Walled Garden
Chollerford, Hexham
Northumberland NE46 4BQ
Tel: 01434 681483

Attractive nursery offers a wide range of herbs and some perennials, and holding the National Collection of marjorams and thymes.

Hillview Hardy Plants
Worfield
Near Bridgnorth
Shropshire WV15 5NT
Tel: 01746 716454
Fax: 01746 716454
email: hillview_hardy_plants@compuserve.com

Large range of auriculas including many hard-to-find cultivars, as well as an interesting selection of hardy perennial plants.

V. H. Humphrey
Westlees Farm, Logmore Lane
Westcott, Dorking
Surrey RH4 3JN
Tel: 01306 889827
Fax: 01306 889371

Iris specialist and National Collection holder offering the widest selection in Britain; many historic varieties are among the 500 offered.

Kingstone Cottage Plants
Kingstone Cottages
Weston under Penyard
Ross on Wye
Herefordshire HR9 7PH
Tel: 01989 565267

Fascinating collection of *Dianthus* offered by National Collection holders: rare old varieties, cottage garden favourites and alpine hybrids.

Lower Icknield Farm Nurseries
Meadle
Princes Risborough
Aylesbury
Bucks HP17 9TX
Tel: 01844 343436

Argyranthemum (marguerite) specalist, holder of the National Collection.

Margery Fish Plant Nursery
East Lambrook Manor
South Petherton
Somerset TA13 5HL
Tel: 01460 240328

Many interesting plants with excellent selection of violas.

Merriments Garden
Hawkhurst Road
Hurst Green
East Sussex TN19 7RA
Tel: 01580 860666

This nursery and 4-acre garden offers a good selection of hardy plants.

Mires Beck Nursery
Low Mill Lane
North Cave, Brough
East Yorkshire HU15 2NR
Tel: 01430 4230 421543

Specialist wildflower grower, concentrating on those originating in Yorkshire.

Monksilver Nursery
Oakington Road
Cottenham
Cambridge CB4 4TW
Tel: 01954 251555
email: monksilver@dial.pipex.com

Extensive range of unusual hardy perennials including excellent selection of perennial sweet peas from *Vinca* National Collection holder.

Paradise Centre
Twinstead Road
Lamarsh
Bures
Suffolk CO8 5EX
Tel: 01787 269449

Nursery and garden, with unusual bulbous and tuberous plants including shade and bog varieties. Herbaceous perennials and over 20 species of *Allium*.

Parigo Horticultural Co Ltd
Newlands Nurseries
Lagness
Chichester
W. Sussex PO20 6LL
Tel: 01243 539937

Wide range of perennials and National Collection of alstroemerias.

Perhill Nurseries
Worcester Road
Great Witley
Worcestershire WR6 6JT
Tel: 01299 896329
Fax: 01299 896990

An interesting range of unusual perennials as well as alpines and herbs.

Perryhill Nurseries
Hartfield
Sussex TN7 4JP
Tel: 01892 770377
Fax: 01892 779029

Wide range of plants including many hard-to-find perennials; also old shrub roses and a good selection of clematis.

The Picton Garden and Old Court Nurseries
Colwall, Malvern
Worcs WR13 6QE
Tel: 01684 540416
Fax: 01684 565314

The nursery offers a very wide range of asters; visit in autumn to view the National Collection of Michaelmas daisies at their best.

Plant World
St Marychurch Road
Newton Abbot
Devon TQ12 4SE
Tel: 01803 872939

Unusual cottage garden plants are included in this nursery's range of plants, and a unique garden plan in the shape of a world map illustrates the origin of plants. Holder of the National Collection of primulas.

Pleasant View Nursery
Two Mile Oak
Newton Abbot
Devon TQ112 6DG
Tel/Fax: 01803 813388

Salvia specialist, and holder of the National Collection.

Rougham Hall Nurseries
A14 Rougham
Bury St Edmunds
Suffolk IP30 9LZ
Tel: 01359 270577   Mobile: 0860 387730
Fax: 01359 271149
email: kelvin-harbutt@msn.com

Wide range of container-grown hardy perennials.

Southview Nurseries
Chequers Lane
Eversley Cross
Hook
Hants RG27 0NT
Tel: 0118 9732206

Old pinks and hardy pinks from holders of a National Collection, plus good herbaceous perennials.

Stenbury Nursery
Smarts Cross
Southford
Near Whitwell
Ventnor, Isle of Wight
Tel: 01983 840115

Daylily specialist.

Stillingfleet Lodge Nurseries
Stillingfleet
York YO4 6HW
Tel: 01904 728506

Unusual perennials including many fragrant and grey foliage plants from the holder of a National Collection of pulmonarias.

Wildflower Nursery
62 Lower Sands
Dymchurch
Romney Marsh
Kent TN29 0NF
Tel: 01303 873052

Wild garden plants and seed, and advice on wildlife habitats. *See page 88.*

Yardley's Devon Violet Nursery
Rattery
South Brent
Devon TQ10 9LG
Tel: 01364 64033

Yorkshire Garden World
Main Road
West Haddesley
Selby
N. Yorkshire YO8 8QA
Tel: 01757 228279

Santolina specialist.

PLACES TO VISIT

This list comprises just a few of the many interesting gardens worth a visit. In addition to all those which hold National Collections (see NCCPG entry page 177), many fascinating gardens are open under The National Gardens Scheme who publish an annual directory (the '"Yellow book") of Open Gardens. Many contain old-fashioned varieties.

The National Trust maintains many gardens of historical interest. Contact them at: 36 Queen Anne's Gate, London SW1H 9AS Tel: 0171 222 9251.

Antony House (National Trust)
Torpoint
Cornwall PL11 2QA
Tel: 01752 812364

The home of Sir John and Lady Cynthia Carew-Pole, stunning gardens include a large National Collection of daylilies. Open Tuesday–Thursday from April to October, Bank holidays, and Sundays from June to August.

Bayleaf garden at the Weald and Downland Open Air Museum
Singleton, Chichester
West Sussex PO18 0EU
Tel: 01243 811348

Interesting re-creation of a 16th century yeoman homestead, using period plants and techniques.

Birmingham University Botanic Gardens
School of Continuing Studies
Winterbourne
58 Edgbaston Park Road, Edgbaston
Birmingham B15 2RT
Tel: 0121 414 5590
Fax: 0121 414 5619

Well-maintained and presented botanic garden including a rose garden of clearly labelled historic roses.

Chelsea Physic Garden
66 Royal Hospital Road
London SW3
Tel: 0171 352 5646

A fascinating historic garden containing many old plants based on those grown in the garden by influential 18th century gardener Philip Miller. Open Wednesday and Sunday afternoons only, from April to October.

Edinburgh Royal Botanic Garden
Inverleith Row
Edinburgh EH3 5LR
Tel: 0131 552 7171

One of the oldest botanic gardens in Britain, with a fine plant collection including a good display of trilliums.

Felbrigg Hall (National Trust)
Roughton
Norwich NR11 8PR
Tel: 01263 837444

The extensive gardens are worth a visit at any time of year but are particularly fine in autumn when visitors can see the fine National Collection of colchicum.

Gravetye Manor Hotel
East Grinstead RH19 4LJ
Tel: 01342 810567
Fax: 01342 810080

William Robinson's own garden, scrupulously maintained, with herbaceous borders, old roses, topiary, woodland garden and alpine meadow. The garden is open to hotel guests and by special arrangement, but the public can walk the perimeter path on Tuesdays and Fridays.

Hodsock Priory
Blyth
Worksop S81 0TY
Tel: 01909 591204
Fax: 01909 591578

Richly planted garden on an ancient moated site, with excellent rose gardens and mixed borders, and spectacular snowdrops and aconites in early Spring. Open Tuesday –Thursday afternoons, April to August, also daily February to March for snowdrops.

The Jephson Gardens
Royal Leamington Spa
Warwickshire
Tel: 01296 425812

Guided tours are available and recommended round this National Collection of digitalis in a municipal park setting.

Kingston Maurward College
Dorchester
Dorset DT2 8PY
Tel: 01305 215000
Fax: 01305 215001

The holders of a National Collection of penstemons and salvias, the Visitor Centre is open daily during summer and some plants are available.

Knightshayes Court
Bolham, Tiverton EX16 7RQ
Tel: 01884 254665

A garden to visit in April and May to enjoy the extensive bulb collection at its best.

Museum of Garden History
The Tradescant Trust
Lambeth Palace Road
London SE1 7LB
Tel: 0171 401 8865

A fascinating museum plus unique 17th century style garden including many plants introduced by the Tradescants. See page 20.

Newby Hall and Gardens
Ripon, North Yorkshire
Tel: 01423 322583

Stunning herbaceous borders as well as a large collection of rare and beautiful shrubs and trees. Plants are offered for sale.

Oxford Botanic Garden
High Street
Oxford OX1 4AX
Tel/fax: 01865 276920

National Collection of euphorbia, in a beautifully laid out, well labelled botanic garden; also fine glasshouses, conifers, herbs, old roses and record size trees. Open daily.

Ripley Castle Gardens
Ripley, Harrogate
North Yorkshire HG3 3AX
Tel: 01423 770152
Fax: 01423 771745

Beautiful gardens are open daily, and include the National Collection of *Hyacinthus orientalis*.

The Rococo Garden
Painswick House, Painswick
Gloucestershire GL6 6TH
Tel: 01452 813204

Historic garden with many period features, famous for its extensive snowdrop woods. The huge collection of snowdrops is associated with the 19th century gardener James Atkins, after whom the tall variety *Galanthus nivalis* 'Atkinsii' is named.

Royal Horticultural Society Gardens
Wisley
Woking
Surrey GU23 6QB
Tel: 01483 224234

Home of National Collections of crocus, epimedium, galanthus, pulmonaria (among others), the 200-acre (80 hectare) gardens delight, instruct and inspire. Highlights include alpine meadows, rock gardens, an alpine house, a woodland garden, glasshouses, mixed borders and model gardens. Open daily.

The Royal National Rose Society
The Gardens of the Rose
Chiswell Green
St Albans
Herts AL2 3NR
Tel: 01727 850461
Fax: 01727 850360

Display of over 1,700 different rose species and cultivars at the Society's headquarters, to which members have free access. Hundreds of new roses in trial fields which can be visited. Pruning demonstrations which anyone can attend.

SELECTED
EUROPEAN NURSERIES

AUSTRIA

Alpengarten Zenz
Rosenheim 5
A-8071 Grambach bei Graz
Austria
Tel: 0043 316 401239

Good source of unusual species and forms of alpine plants plus annuals and herbaceous plants.

Stauden Feldweber
Im Innkreis 139
A-4974 Ort
Bahnhof St Martin/Innkreis
Austria
Tel: 0043 7751 320
Fax: 0043 7751 7223

Wide range of alpine plants and hardy perennials.

Praskac Pflanzenland
Baumschulen Staudenkulturen
Gartenzentrum Gartengestaltung
Praskacstrasse 101–108
3430 Tunil/Donau
Austria
Tel: 0043 2272 62460
Fax: 0043 2272 63816

A famous Austrian nursery offering a wide range of excellent herbaceous perennials, plus shrubs and trees.

Sarastro
Christian Kress
A-4974
Ort in Immkreis
Austria
Tel: 0043 7751 3685
Fax: 0043 4248 3688

Wide range of herbaceous perennials.

Silvia Tunkl
Hauptplatz 8
A-2242 Prottes
Austria
Tel: 0043 2282 3958
Fax: 0043 2282 5178

Range of Mediterranean and exotic plants and seeds, including large selection of passifloras.

BELGIUM

Koen Engelen
Wijnegembaan
B-2520 Ranst
Tel: 0031 3 3540270
Fax: 0031 3 3530158

Iris specialist – hundreds of iris of every type and form.

Lens Roses
Redinnerstraat 11
B-8460 Oudenburg
Belgium
Tel: 0032 59267 830
fax 0032 59265 614

Large number of old-fashioned and shrub roses as well as modern types.

FRANCE

Gaec de Champagne M Bourdillon
B P 2
F-41230 Soings en Solonge
Tel: 0033 25498 7106
Fax: 0033 25498 7676

Specialist in irises and daylilies.

Bernard Boureau
28 bis, rue de Maréchal Galliéni BP8
F-77166
Grisy-Suisnes
France
Tel: 0033 16405 9183
Fax: 0033 16405 9766

Large collection of roses, plus display gardens with more than 400 old roses.

Cayeux
Boite Postale 35
F-5501
Gien Cedex
France
Tel: 0033 0238 670508
Fax: 0033 0238 678498

Breeders of a huge range of iris.

Les Roses Anciennes d' André Eve
Lieu-dit Morailles
F-45300
BP 206 Pithiviers-le-Vieil
France
Tel: 0033 23830 0130

Extensive collection of old-fashioned roses plus some modern ones.

Pépinières Filippi
Route Nationale 113
F-34140 Mèze
France
Tel: 0033 46743 8869
Fax: 0033 46743 8459

Mediterranean plant specialist.

Roseraies Pierre Guillot
Domaine de la Plaine
F-38460 Chamagnieu
France
Tel: 0033 47490 2755
Fax: 0033 47490 2717

Rose breeders and growers since the early 19th century.

Lumen
Les Coutets
F-24100
Creysse Bergerac
France
Tel: 0033 55357 6215
Fax: 0033 55358 5488

Wide range of quality perennials including full range of cottage garden herbaceous plants.

Santonine
Tout y Faut
F-17260 Villars en Pons
Tel: 0033 54694 2694
Fax: 0033 54694 6236

Excellent list of herbaceous perennials.

Pépinières Travers
Rue Cour-Chaerette
F-45650 Saint Jean le Blanc
Tel: 0033 23866 3753
Fax: 0033 23851 9018

Climbing plants, including a wide range of clematis.

Pépiniére Botanique Jean Thoby
Château de Gaucajq
F-40330 Amou
Tel: 0033 55889 2422
fax 0033 55889 0662

Over 500 varieties of camellias, plus an extensive range of climbers and perennials.

GERMANY

Ingwer J Jensen GMBH
Am Schloßpark 2B
D-264960 Glucksberg
Germany
Tel: 0049 4631 60100

Large collection of roses and climbers.

Staudengärtnerei Heinz Klose
Rosenstrasse 10
D-34253 Lohfelden bei Kassel
Germany
Tel: 0049 561 515555
Fax: 00 49 561 515120

Specialises in paeonies, hostas, delphiniums and herbaceous perennials.

W Kordes & Söhne
D-25365 Klein Offenseth-Sparrieshoup
Tel: 0049 4121 48700
Fax: 0049 4121 84745

One of the largest rose specialists in Europe, offering many home bred roses plus a number of good old-fashioned cultivars.

Osnabrücker Staudtenkulturen
Linner Kirchweg 2
D-49143 Bissendorf-Linne
Germany
Tel: 0049 5402 5618
Fax: 0049 5402 4706

Specialising in herbaceous perennials and phlox.

Naturwuchs Gartnerei
Bardenhorst 15
D-33739 Bielefeld-Vilsendorf
Germany
Tel: 0052 1875 1500

Shrubs, roses and perennials.

Rosen von Schultheis
Rosenhof
D-61231 Bad Neuheim Steinfurth
Tel: 0049 6032 81013
Fax: 0049 6032 85890

Run by the same family for well over a century, Schultheis specialises in old and rare roses.

Staudenkulturen Stade
Beckenstrang 24
D-46325 Borken-Marbreck
Tel: 0049 2861 2604

Wide range of herbaceous perennials.

Botanischer Alpengarten F Sundermann
Aeschacher Ufer 48
D-88131 Lindau/Bayern
Germany
Tel: 0049 8382 5402
Fax: 0049 8382 21539

Excellent range of traditional alpines.

Tausendschön
Haupstrasse 19
D-74541 Vellberg-Großaltdorf
Germany
Tel: 0049 7907 89792
Fax: 0049 7907 23865

Old-fashioned roses and wide range of herbaceous plants.

Gartenbau F Westphal
Peiner Hof 7
D-25497 Prisdorf
Germany
Tel: 0049 4101 74104
Fax: 0049 4101 781113

Clematis specialist.

Bernard und Gabriele Wetzel
Meisterbetrieb
Kohlfurther Strasse 141
D-42349 Wuppertal-Cronenberg
Tel: 0202 4704 43
Fax: 0202 47801 19

Rare plants, specialising in orchids.

Staudengärtnerei Gräfin von Zeppelin
Laufen bei Staufen (Sudbaden)
D-79295 Sulzburg
Baden
00 49 7634 69716
fax: 00 49 7634 6599

Specialises in herbaceous perennials, iris, paeonies and
Oriental poppies.

ITALY

Cellarina di Maria Luisa Sotti
Via Monta 65
1-14100 Cellarengo
Tel: 0039 141 935258
Fax: 0039 141 935258

Wide range of aromatic and scented plants as well as grey
leaved perennials.

Rose Barni
Via Autostrada 5
1-51100 Pistoia
Tel: 0039 573 380464
Fax: 0039 573 382072

Famous old firm of rose breeders, introducers and growers.

Venzano
Loc Venzano
Mazzolla
1-56048 Volterra
Tel: 0039 588 39095
Fax: 0039 588 39095

Specialising in aromatic and scented plants, including
many old pinks and scented pelargoniums.

Vivaio Guido degl'Innocenti
Via Colle Ramole
7 Loc Bottai
1-50029
Tel: 0055 237 45 47
Fax: 0055 202 06 76

Large selection of irises and hemerocallis.

Walter Branchi
Le Rose
Corbara 55
1-05019 Orvieto

Probably the most complete list of 19th century roses in
the world.

THE NETHERLANDS

Belle Epoque Rozenkwerkerij
Oosteinderweg 489
NL 1432 BJ
Aalsmeer
Tel: 0031 297 342546
Fax: 0031 297 340597

The most comprehensive rose list in Holland.

Coen Jansen
Ankummer Es 15
NL 7722 RD
Dalsen
Tel: 0031 5294 34086

Wide range of herbaceous plants including many unusual
cultivars.

Pieter Zwijneburg
Halve Raak 18
NL 2771 AD
Boskoop
Tel: 0031 172 216232
Fax: 0031 172 218474

Huge selection of herbaceous plants as well as trees and
shrubs, many unusual plants.

BIBLIOGRAPHY

Andersen Horticultural Library's Source List of Plants and Seeds, Andersen Horticultural Library, University of Minnesota, 1996

Creating a Wildflower Garden, Jonathan Andrews, Henry Holt & Co, New York, 1986

Thomas Jefferson's Flower Garden at Monticello, Edwin M. Betts and Hazlehurst Bolton Perkins, The University Press of Virginia, Charlottesville, 1986

The Standard Cyclopedia of Horticulture, L. H. Bailey , The Macmillan Company, New York, 1956

New Book of Flowers, Joseph Beck, Orange Judd Company, New York, 1879

RHS A-Z Encyclopedia of Garden Plants, ed Christopher Brickell, Dorling Kindersley, London, 1996

The Vanishing Garden, Christopher Brickell and Fay Sharman, John Murray, London, 1986

Flowers and their Histories, Alice M Coats, McGraw-Hill Book Company, New York, 1956

The History and Folklore of North American Wildflowers, Timothy Coffey, Houghton Mifflin Company, New York, 1994

Lys de Bray's Manual of Old-Fashioned Flowers, Lys de Bray, The Oxford Illustrated Press, Sparkford, Somerset, 1984

The Origins of Garden Plants, John Fisher, Constable and Company Ltd, London, 1982

The Heirloom Garden, Jo Ann Gardner, Garden Way PublishingVermont, 1992

The Cottage Garden and the Old-Fashioned Flowers, Roy Genders, Pelham Books, London, 1969

Country Herbal, Lesley A Gordon, Gallery Books, New York, 1984

The Development of Garden Flowers, Richard Gorer, Eyre and Spottiswoode Ltd, Great Britain, 1970

The New Royal Horticultural Society Dictionary Index of Garden Plants, Mark Griffiths, Timber Press, Portland, Oregon, 1994

Early Gardening Catalogues, John Harvey, Phillimore, Sussex, 1972

Early Nurserymen, John Harvey, Phillimore, Sussex, 1974

Green Immigrants, Claire Shaver Haughton, Harcourt Brace Jovanovich, New York, 1978

The Sunflower, Charles B. Heiser Jr, University of Oklahoma Press, OK, 1976

Henderson's Handbook of Plants, Peter Henderson, Peter Henderson & Company, New York, 1881

English Cottage Gardens, Edward Hyams, Penguin Books Ltd, Middlesex, England, 1970

Geoff Hamilton's Cottage Gardens, Geoff Hamilton, BBC Books, London, 1995

Plants in Garden History, Penelope Hobhouse, Pavilion Books, London, 1997

Flower Chronicles, Buckner Hollingsworth, Rutgers University Press, New Jersey, 1958

The Oxford Companion to Gardens, eds Geoffrey Jellicoe, Susan Jellicoe, Patrick Goode, Michael Lancaster, Oxford University Press, Oxford and New York, 1991

Garden Plan: A Detailed Guide to the Museum of Garden History's 17th Century Style Garden, Anne Jennings, The Tradescant Trust, London, 1996

Wildflowers Across America, Lady Bird Johnson, and Carlton B Lees, Abbeville Press, New York, 1988

Cottage Garden Annuals, Clive Lane, David and Charles, Devon, 1997

Early American Gardens: "For Meate or Medicine", Ann Leighton, Houghton Mifflin Company, Boston, 1966

Once Upon a Windowsill, Tovah Martin, Timber Press, Portland, Oregon, 1988

Flora Britannica, Richard Mabey, Chatto & Windus, London, 1996

Where Have all the Wildflowers Gone? Robert H Mohlenbrock, Macmillan Publishing Co, Inc., New York, 1983

Popular Annuals of North America 1865–1914, Peggy Cornett Newcomb, Dunbarton Oaks Research Library and Collection, Washington DC, 1985

The Illustrated Dictionary of Gardening, George Nicholson, James Penman, New York, 1887

Bulbs, Roger Phillips and Martyn Rix, Pan Books, London, 1989

Rhodora: the Journal of the New England Botanical Club Vol. 98, No. 895, Summer 1996

Roots: Journal of the Historical Iris Preservation Society Vol. 2, Issue 1, Spring 1989

The Plant Finder, The Royal Horticultural Society, 1997

Myths and Legends of Flowers, Trees, Fruits and Plants, Charles M Skinner, J. B. Lippincott Company, Philadelphia, 1939

Pioneer American Gardening, Elvinia Slosson, Coward-McCann, Inc, New York, 1951

Heritage Vegetables, Sue Stickland, Gaia Books, London 1998

Plants from the Past, David Stuart and James Sutherland, Viking Penguin Books Ltd, England, 1987

Heirloom Vegetable Gardening, William Woys Weaver, Henry Holt and Company, 1997

Heirlooms and Genetics, Lyman N White, Lyman N. White, Cambridge, NY, 1988

Fascinating information was also gleaned from many specialist magazines and newsletters, particularly from numerous issues of *The Garden* (the journal of the Royal Horticultural Society), *Gardens Illustrated,* the NCCPG publication *Plant Heritage,* and *Plantlife,* the magazine of the British wild plant conservation charity.

INDEX

For common names not listed below, please see the Contents list on pages 102–3.

PUBLISHER'S ACKNOWLEDGEMENTS

Gaia Books would like to thank everybody who helped by providing information for this project, even though we were unable to use it all: particularly Derek and Judy Tolman, Clive Gandley, E Bullock, Dr JR Burwell, Mrs P. Davies, Michael and Sophie Hughes, Caroline Atkinson, TM Upson, Parigo Horticultural Co Ltd, Dr JD Twibell, Paul and Meriel Picton, Dr RJ Gornall, Mrs L M Williams, Peter and Susan Lewis, Dr A G Dickinson, R Cobb, KG Harbutt, M Marshall, Sarah Franklyn, M and S Hughes, M and E Trenear, TA Baker, Noreen Jardine, Lynn Raynor,

K Pratt, TM Upson, D Bromley, Mrs A Christie, A Norton, Judith Bradshaw, Mr and Mrs A Mallett, MA Sandell, Wood, Valerie Anderson, Dr RJ Gornall, AK Shipp, Ripley Castle Estate Office, KW Davis, Miss S Norton, Chris and Judy Yates, G Mawson, Pamela Taylor, Pat Edwards, Jean Sambrook, R Brown, M Harwood, M Bristow, J N D'Arcy, P Nicholls, Margaret Baber, M Thrower, DL Dean, Kingston Maurward gardens, SP Keeble, LA Allen, Ray Brown, Mrs Vanessa Cook, Lieut Col KJ Grapes, M Baldwin, J Bates, Professor JG Hawkes,

Pandora Thoresby, Mr and Mrs BD Yeo, Mrs CA Atkinson, Sylvia Parrett, E and R Heaton, Mrs KA White, C Denton, D Bromley, Peter and Janet Foulsham, LA Salt, Mrs YS Matthews, Johanna Westgate, and the many nurseries who sent catalogues.

    Thanks also to Barbara Segall for her tireless assistance, to Lynn Bresler for compiling the Index, to Julia Rowntree for her illustration on pages 11 and 99, and to Caroline Sheldrick for research and copyediting.

ALSO PUBLISHED BY GAIA BOOKS

HERITAGE VEGETABLES
Sue Stickland

£14.99

ISBN 1 85675 033 7

How and why to save and exchange old-fashioned vegetable seeds as part of our heritage. This book also gives practical advice on cultivation and recommends vegetable varieties for their flavour and their suitability for specific soils and aspects.

THE NATURAL GARDEN
Peter Harper with Jeremy Light and Chris Madsen

£18.99 h/b   ISBN 1 85675 085 X
£14.99 p/b   ISBN 1 85675 056 6

A fresh, practical guide to gardening in harmony with nature. Learn organic, biodynamic and permaculture techniques through illustrations, charts and detailed instructions, and create a healthy and productive garden.

THE ROTHSCHILD GARDENS
Miriam Rothschild, Lionel de Rothschild and Kate Garton

£25.00

ISBN 1 85675 092 2

This book leads you through some of the most stunning gardens in Europe, created and managed by one of Europe's most powerful families, from the elegant grace of Waddesdon to the author's own beautiful wildflower garden, Ashton Wold.

THE COMPLETE FLORAL HEALER
Anne McIntyre

£15.99

ISBN 1 85675 067 1

People have known for centuries that flowers can be used to cure ailments. This book contains descriptions of the healing properties of each flower featured as well as a guide to Bach Flower Remedies, Australian Bush Remedies and Californian Flower Essences. It includes full colour photographs and artwork.

EARTH TO SPIRIT
David Pearson

£11.99

ISBN 1 85675 046 9

In the past, buildings expressed a harmony between people, land and cosmos that linked Earth to Spirit. Pearson explores new architecture that honours old traditions yet uplifts them with current ideas - from home and garden to community design.

HEART AND HOME
Beverly Pagram

£14.99

ISBN 1 85675 054 X

Escape from the pressures of everyday life by making your home into a sensual cocoon of colour, light, sounds, textures and smells with this highly illustrated book. Decorating ideas that allow you to reflect your personality in your home.

To order any of these books direct from the publisher or to request a full catalogue of titles published by Gaia Books please call 01453 752985, fax 01453 752987 or write to Gaia Books Ltd., 20 High Street, Stroud, Gloucestershire, GL5 1AZ e-mail address info@gaiabooks.co.uk Internet address http://www.gaiabooks.co.uk